Reference Skills for the School Library Media Specialist: Tools and Tips

Ann Marlow Riedling

Linworth Publishing, Inc.
Worthington, Ohio

Cataloging-in-Publication Data
Riedling, Ann Marlow, 1952-
    Reference skills for the school library media specialist : tools and tips / Ann Marlow Riedling.
    p. cm.
    Includes bibliographical references (p.) and index.
    ISBN 1-58683-000-7
1. School libraries--Reference services--United States. 2. Instructional materials
    centers--United States. I. Title.

Z675.S3 R54 2000
025.5'2778--dc21

                                                            00-042127

Published by Linworth Publishing, Inc.
480 East Wilson Bridge Road, Suite L
Worthington, Ohio 43085

ISBN 1-58683-000-7

5 4 3 2 1

Table of Contents

Table of Contents continued

Table of Contents continued

Preface

Reference Skills for the School Library Media Specialist: Tools and Tips is designed for courses that prepare college and university students for undergraduate or graduate degrees in school library media. Its objectives are to teach basic reference processes, sources, services, and skills and to provide authentic school library media reference scenarios for reflection and guided application.

Few textbooks have been written concerning reference sources and services that are *geared specifically and appropriately for the school library media specialist*. With the ever-changing role of the school library media specialist, the area of reference has also seen major alterations and adjustments—the infusion of innovations, in particular, new technologies. This book addresses current issues and concepts of reference sources and services as they concern today's library media specialists. This text includes references to the most recent AASL guidelines, *Information Power: Building Partnerships for Learning*. School library media specialists should be influential in fostering effective and efficient access, evaluation, and use of information. They are in a prime position to deliver this information by teaching students to become information-literate in our global society.

This textbook is a practical manual. It offers current basic reference information along with practical examples to give prospective library media specialists insight into the numerous situations that arise in school library media centers.

The manual is divided into five parts.

- *Part I: What Is Reference All About?* discusses reference processes, sources, and services, focusing on the human side of reference work. It addresses significant school library media reference terminology, techniques, and concepts. Additionally, research processes and models such as the *Big6*™ by Eisenberg and Berkowitz, *Information Seeking* by Kuhlthau, and the *Research Process* by Stripling and Pitts are outlined. Selection, evaluation, and maintenance of the reference collection are also discussed in *Part I*—methods and sources of discovering the appropriate print and electronic reference materials for the school library media situation, as well as effective organization of the collection.

- *Part II: Nuts and Bolts* speaks about the actual types of reference sources used in modern school library media centers, including bibliographies, directories, almanacs, yearbooks, handbooks, biographical sources, dictionaries, encyclopedias, geographical sources, indexes, and abstracts. Print and electronic sources are not addressed separately, but occur together throughout the chapters, as electronic resources are prevalent in today's reference world.

- *Part III: The Art of Questioning* discusses the reference interview. This valuable conversation between the student and the school library media specialist connects knowledge with information needs. Effective communication is a critical component of school library media reference services.

- *Part IV: Reference for the New Millennium:* Our evolving world includes an incredible growth of knowledge, an explosion of technology, and a speedy reconfiguration of the boundaries that separate the myriad academic fields and social conventions. Collectively, and with the use of technologies that have brought about this momentum of change, humanity generates enormous amounts of information. The abilities to access, comprehend, evaluate, and use information are skills students must develop in order to function in our current world. *Part IV* specifically addresses modern technological transformations and takes a glimpse into the future, as we move beyond the year 2000 in school library media.

■ *Part V: Scenarios: Situations, Problems, and Solutions* consists of practical scenarios—a look into the real world of school library media reference services. These chapters are divided into elementary, middle, and high school levels, encompassing both large and small school library media centers in both urban and rural settings. The situations include both practical and philosophical aspects of reference services for library media specialists. The scenarios are meant to be read thoughtfully, pondered, and discussed with other prospective or experienced school library media specialists. Following each situation is a list of questions for consideration and reflection. It is hoped that these readings, through guided instruction, will promote thoughtful conversations that will search the very heart of reference services for school library media specialists of the 21st century.

Acknowledgments

I wrote *Reference Skills for the School Library Media Specialist: Tools and Tips* while serving a Fulbright Scholarship in Bahrain. There are numerous people I would like to thank for their continued support, advice, guidance, and insight. With great appreciation, I thank Dr. Judi Repman, my editor, for her ongoing assistance, encouragement, and patience throughout this project. Additionally, many thanks to the numerous other editors who reviewed and read all or portions of the manuscript during its gestation period.

Several school library media specialists "at home" made writing this textbook a much easier task. A special thanks to Mrs. Susan Melcher, library media specialist at Hawthorne Elementary in Louisville, Kentucky, a major source of valuable information as well as a close friend. Others who offered a variety of materials and assistance are Mrs. Susan Elin, library media specialist at Ballard High School, Louisville, Kentucky; Mrs. Jean Noe, library media specialist at New Albany High School, New Albany, Indiana; and Mrs. Carrie Wilberding, library media specialist at Floyd Central High School, Floyds Knobs, Indiana.

Numerous individuals in Bahrain also provided generous assistance. My sincere appreciation goes to Mr. Warwick Price, Director of Library and Information Services, University of Bahrain, and his wife, Linda, who live the true meaning of friendship and caring. I would also like to thank Mrs. Ann Marsh, library media specialist at the Bahrain School; Mrs. Wiesia Thomas of St. Christopher's School; and Mrs. Patricia Sircy, librarian, United States Naval Support Unit, Bahrain.

Most of all, I express my deepest gratitude to my family. My father, who sadly passed away only months ago, and my mother are the foundation that provided me with ongoing strength and courage. Russ, my husband, helped me in too many ways to count; he is my source of inspiration. My daughter, Marlow, shared the "Bahrain experience" with me for 10 months. She is my energy and hope, continually supplying me with support, encouragement, and love. Without them this book would not have been possible.

To all of these people—and many others—I thank you.

I dedicate this book to my father, a true believer in libraries, a man of knowledge, wisdom, and love.

About the Author

Ann Marlow Riedling is a graduate of Indiana University with a B.S. in education; graduate of the University of Georgia with a master's degree and post-graduate work in library science/educational technology as well as post-graduate work at the University of Louisville; and graduate of the University of Louisville with a doctorate in administration and information technology. She has worked in library science and educational technology since 1974: as a resource library media specialist (all grades); media production coordinator; director of a public library; library media specialist in elementary (one year), middle (two years), and high school (10 years); and professor and department chair of Educational Media Librarianship at Spalding University in Kentucky.

PART 1

What is Reference All About?

Chapter *1*

Reference and the School Library: An Overview

Introduction

It is said that there exists a university library in the United States that has carved over its front entrance, "The half of knowledge is knowing where to find it." School library media reference services, in the past, as now, assist students to get better value from the library media collection than they could on their own. Reference for school library media specialists is more than a skilled technique. It is a profoundly human activity ministering to one of the most basic human needs—the desire to know. Reference processes, sources, and services revolve around the principle of maximization of resources underlying all reference work.

Reference Services

What the library media specialist does with regard to reference services is fundamentally to answer questions. The library media specialist must be able to translate questions into terms that align with proper resources—the skill to deliver what are known as reference services. As Kenneth Whittaker explains "The purpose of reference and information service is to align information to flow efficiently from information sources to those who need it. Without the [school library media specialist] bringing source and [student] together, the flow would either never take place at all or only take place inefficiently" (49). The library media specialist acts as mediator between the perplexed student and too much or too little information. As a mediator, the library media specialist weighs the good, the bad, and the indifferent to locate accurate sources to meet students' information needs. The library media specialist helps students determine what they need out of the ever-growing masses of print and electronic information.

Successful library media specialist reference services consist of three components:

■ Knowledge of the library media collection;

■ Effective conversational skills "communication;" and

■ Competence in selecting, acquiring, and evaluating resources to meet students' needs.

Corresponding with these three components are two basic functions of library media center services:

■ The provision of information and

■ Instruction or guidance in the use of information sources.

The American Library Association explains that library media centers exist for the purpose of information and enlightenment. They are institutions with an educational *[instruction]* and informational *[provision of information]* purpose.

The accurate, appropriate provision of information will occur when the library media specialist knows the library media center collection completely and accurately and is competent in selecting, acquiring, and evaluating that collection.

School library media collections consist of a variety of resources. What is a resource? A resource is any source or material, regardless of form or location, that provides necessary answers. *Information Power's Learning and Teaching Principles* says the library media center should provide "access to the full range of information resources" (58). It further states that the library media center should "offer a full range of instructional and informational resources that all students need to meet their curriculum goals" (90). (Evaluation and selection processes and techniques are discussed in the following chapter.)

Instruction in the use of information sources by the library media specialist depends on effective communication. The library media center has been called an "agency of communication." It is important that the library media specialist never lose site of the fact that, to the student, the question is only partly a technical requirement; at a deeper level it is required to satisfy a basic cognitive need. (Chapter 9 addresses communication skills and techniques in more detail.)

Reference services teach or direct students to locate information themselves, giving them an understanding of reference tools and techniques, how to use them, and how the library media center and information are organized. Instructional services also help students to identify and select appropriate materials about a given topic. Instruction or guidance may occur with individuals or groups; however, the end result remains the same—educating students in the use and organization of reference sources and services. It is important to realize that school library media specialists lead students to information, not knowledge. Students manipulate information and construct knowledge from that information. (Research and problem-solving processes and models are addressed later in this chapter.) Another often-overlooked component of instructional service includes orientation to the school library media center. The library media specialist orients students to the organization and scope of the library media center's resources. Orientation may also be a means of welcoming students and encouraging them to visit the library media center.

Reference instruction is also termed *bibliographic instruction,* an expression widely used and accepted in the modern library world and defined as any activity designed to teach students how to locate and use information. Bibliographic instruction goes beyond the physical boundaries of the library media center. With the explosion of technologies that exist within and beyond the walls of library media centers today, the term bibliographic instruction more accurately defines what school library media specialists do with regard to reference work and educating today's students.

The Reference Process

The day of seeking answers has not ended; only the process has changed. What is the reference process? Fundamentally, it consists of the entire transaction with the student in the course of which the reference work is carried out. It contains *three primary elements:* the information, the student, and the answer. These elements combine with *five specific steps* to complete the reference process:

- A need for information,
- A question,
- The search for information,
- An answer or response, and
- An evaluation.

(Figure 1.1 on page 9 more thoroughly explains these five steps in the reference process.)

The reference process may be simply explained as problem solving. The solution to the student's problem is the real object of the process. As fixed as this process may appear, library media specialists must remember that since each question is unique, each process will be unique as well. The reference process is merely an outline; what occurs "within the text" differs from situation to situation and student to student.

Reference and Information Literacy

In today's technological, global society, one aspect of school library media reference services cannot be overlooked: *information literacy.* The bedrock aim of school reference service is to encourage self-help, or information literacy. The *American Library Association* states that information-literate students are "people who have learned how to learn. They know how to learn because they know how knowledge is organized, how to find information.... They are people prepared for lifelong learning" (7). The abilities to access, comprehend, evaluate, and use information have become the skills people must develop in order to function in our world.

Information Power's Information Literacy Standards for Student Learning states that in today's society, the information-literate student "accesses information efficiently and effectively..., evaluates information critically and competently..., [and] uses information accurately and creatively..." (8). (Figure 1.2 on page 10 more completely explains the information literacy process as it relates to student learning.) School library media reference services are particularly important in fostering information literacy through the provision of information, instruction, and guidance.

Research and Problem-Solving Processes and Models

Our complex global society continues to expand at a rate beyond our capacity to comprehend. Access to, comprehension, evaluation, and use of information are needed to ease the burden of change and assist humanity in navigating its course towards the future. It is imperative that students possess the skills to learn efficiently and effectively. Explicitly discussing research and problem-solving strategies makes it more likely that students will transfer these processes to future research and problem-solving situations.

The following three processes or models are widely accepted and used as problem-solving strategies in schools today: *Information Seeking* by Carol Kuhlthau, the *Big6™ Information Problem-Solving Model* by Michael Eisenberg and Robert Berkowitz, and the *Research Process* by Barbara Stripling and Judy Pitts. (Figure 1.3 on page 11 provides a brief overview of these three models.)

Carol Kuhlthau's six-stage model of the information-seeking process conceptualizes how meaning is learned through active participation with information resources. This model encourages an in-depth focus that enables students to seek more relevant information and produce a higher-quality product. Kuhlthau states, "Living in the information age requires people to go beyond the ability to locate information and requires competence in seeking meaning and understanding. More is not necessarily better without skillful guidance from an insightful person [library media specialist]" (708). (Figure 1.4 on page 11 displays this process as it relates to affective, cognitive, and sensorimotor learning.)

Another current, well-known information problem-solving model is the *Big6* approach (www.Big6.com) by Eisenberg and Berkowitz. This process describes the six thinking steps one goes through any time there is an information problem to be solved. Michael Eisenberg explains it this way: "'Brainstorm and narrow' is the essential process for information seeking strategies.... [Students should] brainstorm all possible information sources to meet the task, and then critically determine the best sources for completing the particular task" (22). (An overview of the *Big6* problem-solving model is displayed in Figure 1.5 on page 12.)

The Research Process, developed by Stripling and Pitts, connects information handling and use with subject matter that is essential for learning to occur. Stripling and Pitts discovered that students have little prior knowledge of the information-seeking process, have fragmented understandings of subject knowledge, and do not understand that their information-seeking knowledge depends on content knowledge and vice versa. As a result, school library media specialists should plan instruction specifically to assist students in attaining these skills. Learning experiences should be viewed holistically, recognizing that one area (e.g., information search process) can support other areas (e.g., content knowledge). As Judy Pitts notes, "There are many different, acceptable paths to the same end. Every...[student seemed] to have a different approach to working on a research assignment and organizing information. Each system worked well, but if everyone had been ordered to use one specific approach, many students would have found themselves incredibly frustrated" (23).

Information Power: Building Partnerships for Learning includes a chapter, "Information Literacy Standards for Student Learning." As explained in *Information Power*, "Information literacy—the ability to find and use information—is the keystone to lifelong learning. Creating a foundation for lifelong learning is at the heart of the school library media program....The school library media specialist can use the information literacy standards for student learning to create and maintain a program for a broad learning community—students, teachers, administrators, parents, and the neighborhood—that will support lifelong learning" (1).

Numerous other information problem-solving and research models and processes have been developed and can be extremely valuable in developing school library media reference services. Information problem-solving and critical thinking

---

The Nine Information Literacy Standards for Student Learning

From Information Power: Building Partnerships for Learning by the American Association of School Librarians and Association for Educational Communications and Technology. Copyright 1998 American Library Association and Association for Educational Communications and Technology. Reprinted by permission of the American Library Association.

Information Literacy

STANDARD 1: The student who is information literate accesses information efficiently and effectively.

STANDARD 2: The student who is information literate evaluates information critically and competently.

STANDARD 3: The student who is information literate uses information accurately and creatively.

Independent Learning

STANDARD 4: The student who is an independent learner is information literate and pursues information related to personal interests.

STANDARD 5: The student who is an independent learner is information literate and appreciates literature and other creative expressions of information.

STANDARD 6: The student who is an independent learner is information literate and strives for excellence in information seeking and knowledge generation.

Social Responsibility

STANDARD 7: The student who contributes positively to the learning community and to society is information literate and recognizes the importance of information to a democratic society.

STANDARD 8: The student who contributes positively to the learning community and to society is information literate and practices ethical behavior in regard to information and information technology.

STANDARD 9: The student who contributes positively to the learning community and to society is information literate and participates effectively in groups to pursue and generate information.

involve the application, analysis, evaluation, and synthesis of information to construct personal meaning. Without this ability, students cannot go beyond the mere collection of information in order to weave information threads together into the creation of knowledge. Our role as school library media specialists is to encourage the appropriate problem-solving research processes, as well as critical thinking, in order to lead students to information. Ultimately self-directed learners lead themselves to knowledge from that information.

Reference and the Technology Connection

Less than two decades ago, information sources were synonymous with print materials. It is now an anomaly to use only printed resources in the realm of reference work. Although reference services are changing in dynamic ways for school library media specialists, their essence—the provision of assistance to students seeking information—remains the same. The process of reference services is changing; the goal (the answer) remains constant. Technologies have made it possible to reach that goal faster and more efficiently.

The rapid growth in availability of information in electronic form is transforming the entire role of the library media specialist and reference services as well. It has created a whole new range of options for finding and delivering the information students want. With all the technologies available to us, why are reference services still needed? They are required to determine, among the tons of information, the ounce the student needs. They are required to help students learn how to access, evaluate, and use information; in other words, learn how to learn, to become *information-literate*. Ironically, technology has actually increased the student's need for assistance and reference services. With this in mind, library media specialists face an opportunity and a challenge—not an easy, but a necessary one—to respond to the technological, societal changes of our times.

Conclusion

Reference work for the school library media specialist consists of diverse activities that can be viewed under the two headings of provision of information and instruction or guidance. What the library media specialist *does* with regard to reference work is to answer questions, to lead students to information. To conduct reference services efficiently, the library media specialist should possess three things: knowledge of the collection; effective communication skills; and competence in selecting, organizing, and evaluating resources. The reference process consists of five basic steps to be used as a guideline when providing reference services: a need for information, a question, a search for information, an answer or response, and an evaluation. The three elements necessary for this process are the information, the student, and the answer. One critical element concerning reference sources and services in our technological society is information literacy. School library media specialists should foster information literacy, defined as the ability to access, comprehend, use, and evaluate information. School library media specialists must help students "learn how to learn," to become lifelong learners.

Reference sources and services are constantly changing in response to new societal and technological developments that make information increasingly important and available. There is no doubt that expanding electronic applications will continue to contribute to the importance of reference services and will arguably enlarge the guidance and instructional role of library media specialists in the years ahead. School library media centers and reference services are intended to enrich society and contribute to students' efforts to live better lives. The challenge is ours.

The Reference Process: Five Basic Steps

1. A need for information
- A request is made.

2. A question
- What problem needs solving? What decision or choice needs to be made?
- What data and insight are required to shed light on the main question? What are the additional questions that will help answer the primary question? What does the student already know? What is missing? What does the student not know?

3. The Search for Information
- Based on the question(s), the student and school library media specialist develop research and problem-solving strategies. Where might the best information lie? What sources are likely to provide the most insight most efficiently? Which resources are reliable? What steps will be required to protect against bias and develop a balanced view? Which sources are the most current?
- Resources are located and identified.

4. An answer or response
- Information is sorted and organized; synthesis should occur.
- Are different resources required? Are additional resources required? Is the information provided complete? Does the student understand the information?
- Is the student information-literate; has he or she learned how to learn?

5. An evaluation
- Has the need or needs been met? Is the reference process complete? Incomplete?

Figure 1.1: The Reference Process: Five Basic Steps

The Information Literacy Process as It Relates to Student Learning

At the onset of the information literacy process, the student will identify a need or problem:
- Be inquisitive about a wide range of topics, issues, and problems.
- Recognize the need for accurate and complete information.
- Brainstorm to focus the topic and formulate research questions.

Once the topic is focused and the questions formulated, the student will seek appropriate resources:
- Identify potential sources of information (print, electronic, community).
- Utilize effective research and problem-solving strategies.
- Evaluate sources for appropriateness (reading level, biases).

After the resources have been identified and evaluated, the student will gather information:
- Read, view, and hear a wide variety of appropriate materials.
- Gain background knowledge about the topic.
- Begin building in-depth knowledge regarding certain aspects of the topic.

As the material is being read, viewed, and heard, the student will analyze information:
- Skim and scan for keywords and major ideas.
- Determine the accuracy, relevance, and reliability of the information.
- Differentiate between fact and opinion, agreement and disagreement.
- Identify biases, points of view, and cultural diversity.

After analyzing the information, the student will interpret and synthesize it:
- Summarize and paraphrase the information.
- Draw conclusions based on collected information.
- Create new information as required to replace inaccurate, misleading information.
- Integrate new information with prior knowledge.
- Logically organize and sequence the information.
- Apply information to critical thinking and problem-solving to complete the task.

After summarizing the information, the student will communicate it:
- Select a presentation format appropriate for the purpose and audience.
- Document sources using an appropriate format.

To properly assess the learning process and identify areas needing further development and practice, the student will evaluate process and product:
- Conduct an ongoing evaluation by revising, improving, and updating the process and product as required.
- Determine if the project and process met defined needs.
- Determine what new skills and knowledge were gained.

Figure 1.2: The Information Literacy Process—As It Relates to Student Learning

Overview of Three Research or Problem-Solving Models or Processes

INFORMATION SEEKING Kuhlthau	BIG6 Eisenberg and Berkowitz	RESEARCH PROCESS Stripling and Pitts
1. Initiate task	1. Identify task	1. Choose broad topic
2. Select topic		2. Overview of topic
		3. Narrow the topic
3. Formulate focus	2. Information seeking strategies	4. Develop purpose
4. Explore		5. Formulate question
		6. Plan for research
5. Collect	3. Locate and access	7. Analyze, evaluate
	4. Use information	8. Evaluate evidence
6. Present	5. Synthesize	9. Make conclusions
7. Assess	6. Evaluate	10. Create, present
		11. Reflect

Figure 1.3: Overview of Three Problem-Solving or Research Models or Processes: Information Seeking Model, Big6 Information Problem-Solving, and Research Process Model

The Information-Seeking Process: Affective, Cognitive, and Sensorimotor Learning

STAGE	Affective	Cognitive	Sensorimotor
1. Task initiation	Uncertainty	General, vague thoughts	Recognizing one's information need
2. Topic selection	Optimism	Scheduling, planning	Identifying one's search problem
3. Exploration	Confusion, frustration	Being informed about topic	Investigating scope of topic
4. Formulation	Ease accompanying clarity	Narrowing of topic focus	Formulating a search question
5. Collection	Sense of direction, confidence	Defining, supporting focus	Gathering notes
6. Presentation	Satisfied or dissatisfied	More focused comprehension	Completing a report

Figure 1.4: Carol Kuhlthau's Information-Seeking Process: Affective, Cognitive, Sensorimotor Learning

Big6 Information Problem-Solving Model

Task Definition
- Define the problem.
- Identify the information needed.
  - These questions should be asked prior to beginning the search:
    What type of information do you need to solve your problem?
    Do you need current or historical materials?
    Do you need many or few sources?

Information Seeking Strategies
- Determine all possible sources.
- Select the best sources.
  - Evaluate possible sources to determine priorities.
  - Determine what sources of information are available.
  - Be cognizant of the need to tailor the amount of information to meet specific needs.

Location and Access
- Locate sources.
- Find information within sources.

Use of Information
- Engage.
- Extract relevant information (requires the majority of time).
  - Note sources used; produce accurate citations.

Synthesis
- Organize information from multiple sources.
- Present the result.

Evaluation
- Judge the result and process.

®1987 Michael B. Eisenberg and Robert E. Berkowitz

Figure 1.5: Overview of the Big6 Information Problem-Solving Model (Michael Eisenberg and Robert Berkowitz)

Chapter 2

Selection, Evaluation, and Maintenance of the Reference Collection

Introduction

How does a school library media specialist know what reference materials are needed in the school library media center? How does he or she know if a reference resource is good, bad, or indifferent? Following the rule of "a good reference source is one that serves to answer a question," the focus of this chapter is effective evaluation and selection of reference resources for school library media centers. In explaining the effective evaluation and selection of reference materials, library media specialists should recall a principle in *Information Power's Information Access and Delivery*: "The collections of the [school library media center] are developed and evaluated collaboratively to support the school's curriculum and to meet the diverse learning needs of students" (90).

What is a reference source? It can be defined as materials, from book to computer to periodical to photograph, designed to be consulted for definite items of information rather than to be examined consecutively. Reference sources can be divided into two main classes:

- Compilations that furnish information directly (encyclopedias, dictionaries, almanacs, handbooks, yearbooks, biographical sources, directories, atlases), and
- Compilations that refer to other sources containing information, merely indicating places in which information can be found (bibliographies and indexes).

Adequate and appropriate evaluation and selection of reference materials involve consideration of specific criteria, aids, or tools that may be useful in collection development. (Both types of reference sources are explained in detail in the following chapters.) School library media specialists have a multitude of tasks; one critical task is the evaluation and selection of reference materials. If the library media specialist lacks the proper tools, expertise, or good judgment to accomplish this task, students' information needs may remain unanswered.

What Do You Need? The Selection Process

Selection is the process of deciding what materials to add to the school library media collection. Making selection decisions involves identifying and assessing evaluative information about reference materials, examining the resources, and providing ways to involve others in the selection process.

Meeting curriculum needs is a major criterion for placing items in the library media center collection. School library media specialists should review textbooks used by all teachers, assess teachers' instructional methods, and be aware of specific research and other assignments they give on a regular basis. One of the most important tasks of a school library media specialist is to help students and teachers find the best materials available to support teaching and learning.

All materials—including reference—should meet the criteria of the library media center selection policy. Selection policies are vital because they explain the process followed and the priorities established before any resource is purchased and placed in the library media center collection. A selection policy will state the selection aids used in choosing resources. Numerous tools or aids exist to help decision-makers review new reference publications. Remember, however, that selection is not completely the responsibility of the school library media specialist. It also belongs to administrators, teachers, students, parents, school boards, and community members. Input from these people is essential for a useful, appropriate reference collection.

A number of tools are available to help the school library media specialist decide which reference resources should be added to the collection. Reviews are critical to suitable evaluation and selection of reference materials. However, the media specialist's informed judgment is equally important. Regardless of the situation, a thorough knowledge of the library media center's existing resources is imperative. There are numerous journals, guidebooks and online sources to help library media specialists with the selection of print and electronic reference materials. Most journals contain reviews of electronic media as well as print sources and include articles, columns, editorials and other information as well. The following are *examples* of effective selection tools or aids:

All grade levels:

- *American Libraries Magazine* (American Library Association), available in both print and online formats (**www.ala.org**), lists outstanding reference sources for small- and medium-sized libraries. The Reference and User Services Association's (RUSA) Reference Sources Committee lists the "best reference materials of the year" online; this list is available with annotations in the May issue of the print version of *American Libraries Magazine*.

- *American Reference Books Annual* (Libraries Unlimited, Inc.), published annually since 1970, is available in print format and includes annotations, reviews, and other commentary useful for evaluation and selection of school library media center reference materials.

- *Booklist* (American Library Association) is issued semimonthly, 22 times per year. It includes "Reference Books Bulletin," which focuses specifically on reference resources for libraries. It reviews current books, videos, and software and provides monthly author and title indexes as well as semiannual cumulative indexes.

- *The Horn Book Magazine* (The Horn Book, Inc.) examines children's resources, including reference materials. *Horn Book* is published six times per year and reviews hardback and paperback books. Reviews include bibliographic information, size, age level, summary of content, and other pertinent information for the selection of elementary materials.

- *Media and Methods* (Media and Methods Institute, Inc), available in print and online formats (**www.media-methods.com**), reviews books, CD-ROMs, databases, and online sources, hardware, and other technologies appropriate for K-12 library media centers.

- *School Library Journal* (Reed Elsevier, Inc), is a leading magazine for school library media specialists. One half of *SLJ* is dedicated to critical reviews of print and electronic resources. *School Library Journal* publishes 12 issues per year; the December copy presents the editor's choices for Best Books of the Year.

- *A Guide to Reference Materials for School Library Media Centers* (Libraries Unlimited, Inc.). This print guide covers more than 2,000 titles and includes age and reading levels, presentation styles, strengths and weaknesses, comparisons with other titles, citations, and reviews.

Primary and elementary grades:

- *Children's Catalog* (H. W. Wilson). Now in its 17th edition, this print-format catalog provides a balanced, wide-ranging annotated list of more than 6,000 of the best fiction and nonfiction books, new and established, written for children from preschool through sixth grade.

- *Elementary School Library Collection: A Guide to Books and Other Media* (Brodart), available in both print and CD-ROM, is a well-respected bibliography of titles for preschool through grade six. The annotated collection of titles is a tool for evaluating and building a collection of children's materials including books, audiovisual material, and microcomputer software.

- *Library Talk* (Linworth Publishing, Inc.) is published for the elementary school library media specialist. This journal includes timely reviews of books, software, and CD-ROMs, written by professionals in the school library media field.

- *Reference Books for Children* (Scarecrow Press), a print publication, evaluates reference works and selection tools; discusses selection criteria; and provides author, title, and subject indexes.

Secondary grades:

- *Books for Young Adults, Grades 9-12* (Brodart). This print resource reviews over 50,000 new and backlist titles. Titles are accessible by awards, starred reviews, publisher series, subject categories, and Dewey classification.

- *The Book Report* (Linworth Publishing, Inc.) is designed for secondary school library media specialists. This journal provides reviews regarding books, software, and CD-ROM resources.

- *The Middle and Junior High School Library Catalog* (H. W. Wilson) *(print format)*, now in its 7th edition, includes grades 5-8. This catalog provides an annotated list of more than 4,200 fiction and nonfiction books published in the United States, Canada, and the United Kingdom.

■ *The Senior High School Library Catalog* (H. W. Wilson), a print resource now in its 15th edition, represents a well-balanced collection of some 5,500 outstanding fiction and nonfiction titles essential to the senior high school library collection (grades 9-12).

Online sources:

■ Reference Center at the Internet Public Library (**http://www.ipl.org/ref**) *The Reference Center at the Internet Public Library online resource allows the user to "ask a reference question" or click on a particular book to browse a specific section of the reference collection.*

■ Reference Desk at Librarians' Index to the Internet (**http://www.lii.org**) *This*

online source is a searchable, annotated subject directory of more than 5,700 Internet resources.

■ Internet Library for Librarians (**http://www.itcompany.com/inforetriever**) *This comprehensive Web database is designed to provide a one-stop shopping center for library media specialists to locate Internet resources related to their profession.*

Additional tools may include selection sources published by the American Library Association (**http://www.ala.org**), the Association for Educational Communications and Technology (**http://www.aect.org**), Gale Research (**http://www.gale.com**), H. W. Wilson (**http://www.hwwilson.com**), and R. R. Bowker (**http://www.bowker.com**). Reviews from professional journals in major academic areas should be considered as well. Reference selection tools help the

academic areas should be considered as well. Reference selection tools help the school library media specialist evaluate sources for possible inclusion in the library media center as well as identify gaps in the reference collection. However, these are merely aids; they can help only if the library media specialist has a complete knowledge of the collection and uses good judgment based on existing resources and community and student needs.

How Do You Know If It's Good? The Evaluation Process

It has been said that a "good" reference source is one that answers questions and that a "bad" reference source is one that fails to answer questions. Still another function of the library media specialist is to continually evaluate the quality of the library media center's reference collection. By using appropriate evaluation tools and criteria, the library media specialist is better able to judge whether a particular source meets the needs of the student population. While evaluation criteria were originally developed for printed sources, the evaluation of electronic information considers many of the same elements, with several added components. As in judging any kind of resource, much is subjective. However, the following criteria (appropriate for both print and electronic information) will help library media specialists to evaluate reference resources that answer students' informational needs:

- *Content Scope*: Identifying the scope of material is the basic breadth-and-depth question: What is covered and in what detail? The scope should reflect the purpose of the source and its intended audience. Has the author or editor accomplished what was intended? How current are the contents? Aspects of scope include subject, geographic, and time period coverage. Evaluating scope includes reviewing topical aspects of the subject on which the resource is focused and noting if there are any key omissions. For printed materials, the statement of purpose is generally found in the preface, introduction, or table of contents; for an electronic site, one should look for the stated purpose on the site, along with any limitations that may apply, and site comprehensiveness. Information about CD-ROMs and DVDs can many times be found in the publisher's or vendor's descriptive materials.

- *Accuracy, Authority, and Bias*: Indicators of authority include the education and experience of the authors, editors, and contributors, as well as the reputation of the publisher or sponsoring agency. It is typically easier to evaluate the authority of printed reference sources, because statements of authorship and lists of references can be more easily identified. On the other hand, it is at times extremely difficult to discover who actually provided the information on an electronic site. Some items to look for include who provided the information, why, and explicit statements of authority. Objectivity and fairness are also important considerations. Does the author or contributor have biases that show? How reliable are the facts? These questions may often be answered by examining the coverage of controversial issues and the balance in coverage given to various subjects. Was the site developed as an advertisement or as scholarly material? The creator of the information may serve as an indicator of biases on electronic sites.

- *Arrangement and Presentation*: Printed sources arrange entries in a particular sequence, such as alphabetical, chronological, or classified. If the sequence is familiar, the user may be able to find the sought-for information directly rather than using an index. The flexibility of the reference source is typically enhanced by the availability of indexes offering different ways to find the information. Physical makeup, binding, illustrations, and layout are concerns with print resources. Presentation issues regarding electronic information include page or site layout, the site's organizational design, and help or example sections. Some things to look for include appropriate audience, use of graphics, navigational links, and a table of contents.

- *Relation to Similar Works*: Newly published material may relate to sources already in your school library media center collection, a factor to be taken into account in assessing its potential value. What will this resource add to the current collection? Regarding electronic materials, it is important to assess the extent to which the content corresponds (time period covered, more information provided).

- *Timeliness, Permanence*: Printed resources are often considered to be out-of-date before they reach the student. All sources should be checked for currency. Sometimes relevant information on an electronic site can be located in a document header or footer. Information to observe includes posting and revision dates, policy statements for information maintenance, and link maintenance. It is also significant to recognize that there is no guarantee that a particular file of information will reside in the same location today as it did yesterday. A good strategy is to note the date and time a site is visited if one plans to use the information and cite the source.

- *Cost*: Too often budget, rather than student need, may determine whether a particular reference source is purchased. The cost of print materials and those in distributed electronic form are similar, in that a copy is acquired for in-house use in the school library media center, and the purchase or subscription price buys unlimited access to the contents of the resource. However, online costs may vary widely. In assessing the cost, the library media specialist must attempt to determine if the price is appropriate in relation to the needs of the students, as well as anticipated frequency and length of use. In the case of electronic materials, it is important to consider the cost of hardware and maintenance as well.

Collection Organization and Maintenance

Accurate arrangement and maintenance of the reference collection are necessary for the media specialist's and students' convenience and ease of use. A reference collection that is unplanned and not weeded periodically may prove ineffective and unresponsive to students' information needs. The library media specialist needs a systematic basis for weeding as well as adding new materials to the reference collection. The library media specialist takes into account what is already in the collection and what is actually needed for effective reference work. Weeding criteria for reference materials are similar to those for the total collection: age and currency of material, frequency of use, relevance, physical condition, format, and space availability. It is more important to have a small but relevant, up-to-date collection than a large collection that is neither useful nor of good quality.

Weeding policies for reference materials follow these basic guidelines:
- Encyclopedias should be replaced every five years (and the old ones *not* sent to a classroom);
- Pure science books (except botany and natural history) are out of date within five years;

- Any books dealing with technology should be replaced every five years (or more often);
- Information on inventions and medicine is dated within five years;
- Psychology, history, business, and education sources become dated in 10 years; and
- Newspapers and magazines should be kept up to five years (although most are now purchased either on CD-ROM or online).

Where should these withdrawn materials go? If resources are weeded due to a change in curriculum, it may be beneficial to relocate them to another library. Otherwise, weeded materials should be destroyed.

Today's school library media center reference collections include sources in a variety of formats, from print materials to online. The library media specialist must decide what format to purchase and whether to obtain particular materials in more than one format. Although varying formats may overlap in content, they may differ in accessibility. School library media specialists have more options than ever to create a reference collection that is adequate and appropriate for the library media center, community, and students served.

Decisions in collection development include whether to buy new titles, buy new editions of titles already in the collection, buy the source in CD-ROM or DVD format, or contract with vendors for online access. Maintaining a diverse reference collection is an ongoing process. Regular inventory is required to identify areas that need to be updated or strengthened.

There are many possible ways to arrange reference materials. The arrangement will depend on the library media center, the students served, and the personal preferences of the library media specialist. Blanche Woolls remarks, "It is time to consider ways to make the entire school the media center" (75). Schools that have adopted a whole-language curriculum and teach curriculum across the school *need* to have reference materials away from the central library collection. However, in this situation, the library media specialist must formulate and implement a plan for keeping track of materials so they can be located quickly and easily. If this isn't feasible, one possibility for grouping materials is to maintain a classified arrangement regardless of type. Another alternative is to assemble types of resources together, such as encyclopedias, directories, ready-reference, and the like. It is difficult, however, to integrate sources requiring special equipment, such as computer workstations. Of primary importance is ease of access to reference materials by the library media specialist and the student population.

Conclusion

In order to create and maintain a school reference collection that meets the informational needs of students, the library media specialist must effectively select and evaluate resources. Several considerations are important:

- Knowing about the school, the school community, and the student population,
- Eliciting the expert advice of other faculty members, drawing on their experience and knowledge, and
- Keeping a record of questions asked and research requests.

Remember that the selection process is highly individual. No two library media specialists are alike; student needs differ from school to school. Pay attention not only to known requests, but also to anticipated demands.

Because of the high cost of many reference materials, effective evaluation of reference resources is critical. Although much judgment is subjective, tools or aids and specific criteria are available to bring objectivity to the process. In our technological world, evaluation is even more complex and diverse—and much more vital. A thorough knowledge of existing resources, as well as the community and school population served, is crucial to successful evaluation of reference materials. The significance of experience and practice can't be denied. As explained by William A. Katz, "In time the beginner becomes a veteran. And veteran [school library media specialists] never quit, or are fired, or die. They simply gain fame as being among the wisest people in the world. One could do worse" (3).

PART 2

Nuts and Bolts

Chapter 3
Bibliographies

Introduction

A bibliography brings order out of chaos. Simply stated, a bibliography is a list of materials. More thorough definitions of the term are:

- The history, identification, or description of writings or publications.
- A list of descriptive or critical works of writing related to a particular subject, period, or author; and
- A list written by an author or printed by a publishing house.

Bibliographies are useful tools. They can tell a user the author of a work, publisher, date of publication, cost, and more. The basic purpose remains the same, whether the format is print or electronic.

Bibliographic control refers to two kinds of access to information, *bibliographic* access (Does the work exist?) and *physical* access (Where can the work be found?). Providing bibliographic and physical access is achieved through *bibliographies*, *library catalogs,* and *bibliographic utilities*. Bibliographies list materials (or parts of materials) regardless of location; library catalogs list works located in a given library (or libraries); bibliographic utilities serve both functions. Bibliographic utilities are information vendors who provide a central database for libraries to catalog, share, and retrieve bibliographic records according to national or international bibliographic standards.

Bibliographies and library catalogs can be *current* or *retrospective*. Current bibliographies and library catalogs list works close to the time they are published. Retrospective bibliographic sources cover materials published earlier.

A *universal bibliography* (although currently nonexistent) *would* include everything published from the beginning through the present. Time, territory, subject, language, or form would not limit it. But access to the world's information is definitely nearer, though it is doubtful that "a complete bibliography" will be seen in the immediate future. However, "almost complete" is a reality. This phenomenon is accomplished by having online access to national bibliographies, an example being the Online Computer Library Center (OCLC) found online at **www.oclc.org** (*OCLC First Search a*t (**www.oclc.org/oclc/menu/fs.htm**).

Bibliographies can be divided into several different types: *national bibliographies, trade bibliographies, library catalogs, union catalogs,* and *subject catalogs.*

- *National bibliographies* list materials published in a particular country and are often government-produced. Current national bibliographies usually appear weekly or monthly with cumulative annual or multiyear editions. The United States national bibliography, called the *National Union Catalog (NUC),* lists all works cataloged by the Library of Congress and other members of the system.

- *Trade bibliographies* are commercial publications that include the necessary information to select and purchase recently published materials. Works such as textbooks, government documents, encyclopedias, and dissertations are not included in trade bibliographies. A well-known bibliography of this type is *Books in Print (BIP)*. *BIP* is limited to books available for purchase and contains only printed books (hardbound and paperback).

- *Library catalogs* list materials in the collection of a particular library (such as a school library media center). Because of advanced technologies, many libraries can now provide this information to both local and remote users. These catalogs may also list the collections of other libraries—school library media centers, public libraries, academic libraries, and others.

Examples of Online Subject Bibliographies

(These can be found via http://www.acs.ucalgary.ca/~dkbrown /lists.html)

- *Brave, Active & Resourceful Females in Picture Books*
  Selected and annotated by Claudia Marrow
- *Cinderella Stories*
  Compiled by Kathy Martin
- *Drum Stories*
  A list of folktales involving drums and other percussion instruments, compiled by Mary Mark
- *Children's Literature on Floods and Natural Disasters*
  Compiled and annotated by Lynn Blinn Pike
- *Fractured Fairy Tales*
  Compiled by Betsy Fraser. These are stories that extend, parody, or re-cast the traditional fairy tale in a new light.
- *Holocaust Literature*
  Joan Kindig has compiled a thorough bibliography for grades 5-8.

- *Jewish Religion and Culture in Children's Books*
  An annotated bibliography compiled by Wendy Betts
- *Latino People, History, and Culture*
  An annotated bibliography compiled by Amy Goldenberg. It includes listings of fiction and nonfiction for children and young adults.
- *Medieval World*
  Several annotated bibliographies to introduce children and young adults to the medieval world and Arthurian legend
- *Multiracial Families in Children's Books*
  This is an annotated bibliography by Wendy Betts.
- *Native American Books*
  Reviews from a Native American perspective

- *Union catalogs* identify the materials held in more than one library. Online, through bibliographic utilities (such as OCLC, RLIN, Internet), it is possible to view holdings in thousands of libraries around the world. The geographic area covered may vary from local to multinational. Two useful examples for school library media situations are *SUNLINK,* a Florida project that enables students to use curriculum and information resources, skills, and strategies to become successful. Universal access stations have been established in 24 Florida schools (**www.sunlink.ucf.edu**). The second, the *Texas Library Connection,* is a statewide technology initiative to provide current, relevant information to school districts (www.tea.state.tx.us/technology/libraries).

- *Subject bibliographies* are lists of materials that relate to a specific topic; they are intended for those researching special areas. Hundreds of subject bibliographies exist; many follow the same pattern of organization and presentation. Various disciplines and large areas of knowledge have their own bibliographies. Examples of online subject bibliographies are provided on page 26.

Evaluation and Selection

In evaluating bibliographies, the criteria are authority, frequency, organization, and scope. *Authority* relates to the qualifications of the compiler or the author. He or she should possess the educational background and academic stature appropriate to a bibliographer. As with all reference areas, reputable publishers of bibliographies exist, such as R. R. Bowker, Brodart, and H. W. Wilson. It is advisable to verify the reputation of lesser known publishers through review tools and aids. A bibliography should be current when this is its purpose. Currency also refers to the time lapse between the date of publication of the listed material and the time it enters the bibliography.

Frequency is most applicable when selecting current bibliographies. Often the same work has a different updating schedule in each of its formats. Bibliographies will vary widely in *organization* or arrangement. However, all bibliographies should be organized in an understandable, user-friendly fashion with indexes that complement the arrangement. In addition, the compiler should offer clear instructions for using the work. Bibliographies must be as complete as possible within their stated purposes. In the introduction or preface, the compiler should state the *scope* of the bibliography. It is also valuable to consult guides to the reference works that give concise and unambiguous descriptions of coverage, accuracy, and intent.

The *selection* of bibliographies for a school library media center situation depends on the needs—both known and anticipated—of the school, community, and student population served. Before selecting a specific bibliography, one should read the introduction and several entries and ask the following questions:

- Does the bibliography meet identified needs?
- Are the directions accurate and the explanations clear?
- Is the coverage inclusive for the intended purposes?
- Is it evident why the items are included in the bibliography?
- Is the bibliography well organized and user friendly?

Remain aware of the overall purpose of bibliographies: to provide information about the availability of materials, their costs, and whether they are recommended (although not all bibliographic tools include this element).

AUTHORITY

- The compilers or authors should possess the academic stature expected of bibliographers.
- There are reputable publishers of bibliographies, for example, Brodart, H.W. Wilson, and R. R. Bowker.
- It is important to verify the reputation of lesser known publishers.

FREQUENCY

- The source should be current, when that is the purpose of the bibliography.
- Note that often the same work has a different updating schedule in each of its formats.

ORGANIZATION

- The source should be organized in a clear, user-friendly fashion, with indexes that complement the arrangement.
- The book should offer explicit instructions about how to use the work.

SCOPE

- The scope should be stated in the introduction or preface.
- There are invaluable guides to reference works that give concise, unambiguous descriptions of coverage, accuracy, and intent.

Basic Sources

There are several well-known, "basic" bibliographies for libraries. It is valuable and helpful to become familiar with these reference tools, although your school library media center situation may not require, nor have the budget, to purchase them.

The *American Book Publishing Record (ABPR)*, published by R. R. Bowker, is a monthly publication that includes complete cataloging records for books as they are published.

The *American Reference Books Annual (ARBA)*, an annual publication by Libraries Unlimited, Inc., analyzes more than 1,500 reference titles published or distributed in the United States and Canada. *ARBA* is comprehensive and includes annotations written by subject experts.

Books in Print® (BIP), published annually in September by R.R. Bowker, is a listing of books available from United States publishers. This bibliography is available online (**www.booksinprint.com**) and in various formats—print, CD-ROM, tape and site license. The *BIP* database contains over 3.5 million book, audio and video titles, and over 200,000 new titles are added annually. The web version is newly enhanced to include Hooks to Holdings™, Stock Inventory levels, Order Download formats, and is updated daily, *Books in Print* (print edition) is updated with the *Books in Print Supplement*™, which appears six months after the main vol-

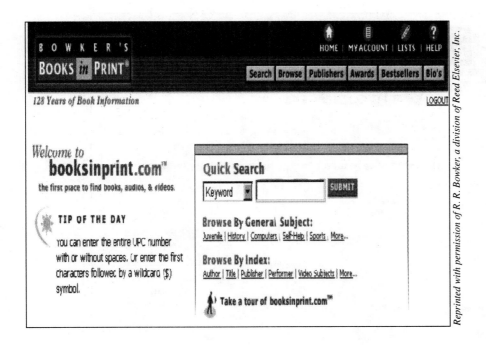

umes of *BIP*. *Children's Books in Print*™ includes 151,000 in-print titles and is published annually. *Forthcoming Books in Print*™ is a bi-monthly supplement that lists new books in print as well as those projected for imminent publication.

Book Review Digest, a quarterly publication, is available online via (**www.hwwilson.com**), in print and CD-ROM formats published by H. W. Wilson. This bibliographic database contains over 62,000 English language fiction and nonfiction titles.

Guide to Reference Books, an American Library Association publication in its 11th edition, lists and annotates over 16,000 titles arranged under main sections; it includes a 400-page index.

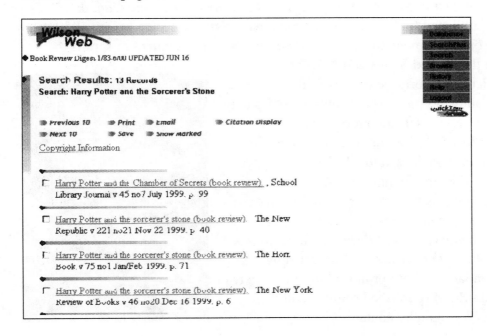

Literary Market Place™ is the directory of American and Canadian book publishing. Now you can have access to *Literary Market Place* and *International Literary Market Place* when you visit (**www.literarymarketplace.com**). Print editions of LMP and ILMP are published annually in the fall.

The *National Union Catalog (NUC)* began as the actual card catalog of the Library of Congress. Later, due to the need for increased access, duplicates of the cards were created, distributed, and maintained by large United States research libraries. The *NUC* can be accessed online via *OCLC First Search* (**www.oclc.org/oclc/menu/fs.htm**); updates vary according to the period covered.

The *Union List of Serials in Libraries of the United States and Canada (ULS) 3rd edition*, published by H. W. Wilson, contains serials published before 1950 in alphabetical order by main entry. As the title indicates, it is limited to serials published in the United States and Canada.

Of particular importance to school library media centers, the following *examples* of bibliographies may also be thought of as "selection tools." There are numerous works of this nature; these are merely a sampling of bibliographies valuable for school library media centers. It is important to purchase these resources carefully, as they are essential for effective collection development.

The Elementary School Library Collection: A Guide to Books and Other Media, published by Brodart, is available in both print (published every two years) and CD-ROM (published semiannually) formats. This bibliography contains 10,000 of the most highly recommended children's titles, preschool through 6th grade. It is compiled by a team of professionals around the country and published every two years. H.W. Wilson's *Children's Catalog* (print format) is an annotated list of more than 6,000 titles for children from preschool through 6th grade. The *Middle and Junior High School Library Catalog, 7th Edition,* and the *Senior High School Library Catalog, 15th Edition,* contain recommended titles for middle and high school students; they are both published by H. W. Wilson. Additional examples of bibliographies suitable for library media center situations are *A to Zoo: Subject Access to Children's Picture Books* (R. R. Bowker*), Best Books for Children* (R. R. Bowker), *Best Books for Young Adult Readers* (R. R. Bowker), and *A Guide to Reference Materials for School Library Media Centers* (Libraries Unlimited, Inc.).

Due to the emergence of new and exciting technologies, numerous bibliographies are available online at no cost. For example, many states have "virtual libraries," online libraries that provide valuable information and are significant resources not to be overlooked for school library media centers. Two other examples of valuable online sources deserve mention:

- *Bookwire* (**www.bookwire.com**), by R. R. Bowker, which claims to be the most comprehensive online information source. It includes timely book industry news, features, reviews, guides to literary events, author interviews, and thousands of annotated links to book-related sites; and
- The *Internet Library for Librarians* (**www.itcompany.com/inforetriever**), which provides information about library vendors, publishers, booksellers, and distributors, as well as an abundance of information regarding specific school library media and reference resources.

A wealth of information is at our fingertips; at times it may seem too much. Bibliographies, however, can organize this data into meaningful, valuable units, eliminating the chaos and bringing order.

Chapter 4

Directories, Almanacs, Yearbooks, and Handbooks

Introduction

One person's trivia are another person's main interest. Directories, almanacs, handbooks, and yearbooks primarily answer ready-reference questions; that is, they're all about facts. A fact book organizes information in a systematic way. As stated in Dickens' *Hard Times*, "Now what I want is facts…. [F]acts alone are wanted in life." A ready-reference question may only take a minute or two to answer; however, the answer could develop into a complex search. For example, a student who requests the address of a specific college may actually want not only the address, but also information about how to apply and other related data. The purpose of this chapter is to provide an overview of these four reference tools, their chief uses, selection procedures, considerations for evaluation, and examples of sources used in school library media centers.

A directory is defined by *The ALA Glossary of Library and Information Science* as "a list of persons or organizations, systematically arranged, usually in alphabetic or classed order, giving address, affiliations, etc. for individuals, and address, officers, functions, and similar data for organizations" (75). This defines a "pure" directory; numerous other ready-reference tools have sections devoted to directory information. Directories are used to locate and verify names of phenomena, as well as to match individuals with organizations. Students often wish to locate other people, experts, organizations, and institutions through names, addresses, phone numbers, ZIP Codes, and titles. Directories are the most rapid and effective method of obtaining this sort of information.

Less obvious uses of directories include limited biographical information about an individual, institution, or political group. Because directories are closely concerned with humans and their organizations, they can serve numerous uses.

Although directories can be divided into a number of categories, the six basic types are government, institutional, investment, local, professional, and trade and business.

Almanacs, yearbooks, and *handbooks* provide factual information about people, organizations, things, current and historical events, countries, governments, and statistical trends. Many other sources also offer this type of information; however, almanacs, yearbooks, and handbooks are more convenient sources. Often they are single volumes that summarize and synthesize large amounts of information.

An *almanac* provides useful data and statistics related to countries, personalities, events, and subjects. It contains astronomical and meteorological data arranged according to days, weeks, and months of a given year, and often includes a miscellany of other information. Almost every school library media center can benefit from having a general almanac. A paperbound edition of many almanacs costs less than $20. The most famous early almanac was Benjamin Franklin's *Poor Richard's Almanac*, published from 1732 to 1748. *Old Farmer's Almanac* is a current example of this type of almanac. Although almanacs can be extensive in geographical coverage, many of the best-known general almanacs are inclined towards a specific country or state. An almanac can answer questions such as

- Where was John F. Kennedy born?
- What is the population of Bahrain?
- Which NCAA Division 1 team has won the most regular season games?
- How much saturated fat is in a pound of lard?
- What is the address of the American embassy in Yemen?

Yearbooks present facts and statistics for a single year (primarily the year preceding the publication date). Encyclopedias often issue yearbooks that supplement the main set and review a specific year. A yearbook's primary purpose is to record the year's activities by country, subject, or specialized area. A general yearbook is the place to find information on topics such as the winner of an athletic event of that year, an obituary for a notable person who died during the year, or the description of a catastrophe that occurred that year.

Handbooks are sometimes called manuals; they serve as guides to a particular subject. Often large amounts of information about a subject are compressed into a single volume. The content and organization of handbooks may vary widely. They are ready-reference sources for given fields of knowledge. Most handbooks have a limited scope. Their particular value is depth of information in a narrow field. There are countless handbooks available; school library media specialists should select specific ones based on ease of arrangement and amount of use. Handbooks provide answers to questions such as

- How do I cite references within the text in APA format?
- Who wrote the poem *The Raven*?
- Is single or double spacing used when writing a formal letter?
- What is the name of the Greek goddess of love?

Facts—answers to ready-reference questions—are a major part of reference services in school library media centers. Ample, suitable resources of this type are essential for any school collection. Although certain factual information can be located in other reference sources, it is always beneficial to have basic directories, almanacs, yearbooks, and handbooks available to meet students' informational needs.

Evaluation of Directories, Almanacs, Yearbooks and Handbooks

SCOPE

- The source should indicate what is covered—organizations, geographic areas, individuals.
- The comprehensiveness of the source should be evident within the stated scope.
- The title and preface should give pertinent information.

CURRENCY

- Note the frequency of the publication and how often it is updated.

ACCURACY

- This is the most important characteristic of works that present factual information.
- Evaluate accuracy by reading reviews, comparing data from different sources, and consulting experts in the field.
- The statistics should be recent and from official, identified sources.

FORMAT

- Entries should be clearly arranged, organized in a logical manner, and consistent throughout the source.
- The index in a fact source should be helpful, accurate, and consistent in style and terminology.
- Electronic sources should offer the advantages of more efficient searching and the ability to combine fields or terms, as well as speed and currency.
- Weigh the advantages against the cost—the major disadvantage of electronic sources.

Evaluation and Selection

The general rules of evaluating any reference work are applicable to directories, almanacs, yearbooks, and handbooks as well. To some degree, we all rely on what reference materials state as facts; however, these should be tested regularly. Is it a fact or an opinion? Is the fact no longer a fact? For instance, at one time in our distant history, it was a "fact" that the world was flat. An effective method of checking a fact is to find its original source. The reference source should clearly indicate where the information came from. The following criteria are useful in evaluating directories, almanacs, yearbooks and handbooks:

- *Scope*: What exactly is covered? What organizations, geographic areas, or types of individuals are included in the resource? How comprehensive is the source within its stated scope? Titles often indicate the scope of the work; the preface will often provide even more detailed information.

- *Currency*: What is the frequency of the publication? How often is it updated? Most reliable are almanacs, yearbooks, and titles that are updated once a year.

- *Accuracy*: Accuracy is the single most important criterion of works that present factual information. How is the information in the source updated? By telephone? Examining public records? Many of these reference resources are composed, entirely or in part, of second-hand information. To test accuracy, one can read reviews, compare data from different sources, and rely on experts in the field. Statistics should be recent and from official sources; those sources should be identified. Reference works without documentation are of questionable validity.

- *Format*: Are the entries clearly arranged, organized in a logical manner, and consistent throughout the source? The index in a fact source should be helpful, accurate, and consistent in style and terminology. A major consideration is the availability of the resource in electronic format (CD-ROM, online). CD-ROMs and online formats may contain more current information than their printed counterparts. Electronic versions can cover a number of years and eliminate the need to consult the numerous volumes. CD-ROMs and online sources can often be searched more efficiently. Keyword searching is helpful; one need not know exact names or titles. Boolean logic enables one to combine fields or terms. The obvious disadvantage of using electronic sources is the cost involved (hardware, software, connect time). This should be weighed against the advantages of speed and the currency of the information

School library media specialists should select all reference sources, including directories, almanacs, yearbooks, and handbooks, with the information requests of students in mind. These types of resources will vary greatly from library media center to library media center. Sources included in a school library media center collection should be based on the students and community served, the types of questions asked, and the number of questions posed in a particular subject area (curriculum needs). Another critical factor in the selection process is the geographic location of the school. This may dictate a concentration of sources dealing with a specific locality. Budget constraints may make it more feasible to buy general sources than specialized directories, almanacs, yearbooks, and handbooks. These four reference tools offer good value at low cost. However, school library media centers generally have smaller collections of this nature than public and larger academic libraries. The age and level of the student population affects the resources selected. As with all reference resources, review journals are invaluable tools in the efficient evaluation and selection of directories, almanacs, yearbooks, and handbooks.

Basic Sources

The *directories, almanacs, yearbooks,* and *handbooks* discussed in this chapter include a *sampling* of the sources appropriate for school library media centers.

Actual selections will depend on your particular school situation. Naturally, these types of resources are not as plentiful nor used as much in elementary levels as they are in secondary library media centers.

Directories. Directories are typically user-friendly reference tools. The scope is normally indicated in the title, and the kind of information is limited and usually presented in an orderly, clear manner. Two obvious and well-used local directories are the telephone book and the city directory. Although offered separately in print format, they are now combined on CD-ROM and online (**www.555-1212.com**). The *National Directory of Addresses and Telephone Numbers* published biannually by Omnigraphics, another directory of this type, contains telephone numbers, fax numbers, addresses, ZIP Codes, and toll-free numbers of more than 120,000 businesses and government agencies in the United States. This directory is available in print and CD-ROM formats. The *AT&T 800 Toll-Free Directory*, published irregularly by AT&T (1992 to present), includes AT&T residential and business toll-free numbers; it is free of charge. This directory is also available online (**www.att.com/tollfree**). Also sponsored by AT&T, the *AnyWho Directory* is yet another useful directory for the location of telephone numbers and related data. By using the online *AnyWho Directory* (**www.anywho.com**), one can locate e-mail addresses, home pages, and toll-free numbers. This directory includes over 90 million entries. *Americom Area Decoder* (**http://decoder.americom.com/**) is another online telephone directory that lets one find an area code by entering a major city name or find a location by entering the area code.

Literary Market Place, published annually by R. R. Bowker, is the ultimate guide to the U.S. book publishing industry. It includes over 4,000 publishers and 12,000 firms directly or indirectly involved with book publishing, covering many aspects of the publishing business. *Literary Market Place* is available in print format (two volumes), on CD-ROM and online (**www.literarymarketplace.com**). *Bookwire* (**www.bookwire.com**), an online source to book-related sites (mentioned in Chapter 3), is also a valuable resource for information regarding book publishing and related topics.

Numerous college and university directories are extremely valuable for secondary school library media centers. Some of the best-known include *Peterson's College Database*, published annually by Peterson's in CD-ROM format (1987 to present); *Peterson's* online version (**www.petersons.com/ugrad**); *Lovejoy's College Guide*, published semiannually by Monarch Press (1949 to present, print format); *Lovejoy's College Counselor*, the CD-ROM equivalent published annually by Intermedia Active Software; and *The College Handbook*, published by the College Board (various dates), available in print format and on CD-ROM. Online college directories include

■ *College Net* (**www.collegenet.com**), which claims to be the number one portal for applying to colleges over the Web and includes over 350 colleges and universities;

■ *All About College* (**www.allaboutcollege.com**), which offers thousands of links to colleges and universities around the world, as well as admissions office e-mail addresses for most schools; and

■ *The Admissions Office* (**www.theadmissionsoffice.com**), which links to hundreds of colleges and universities and offers "LISA" (Live Internet Selection Assistance), a college counselor who provides short answers to general questions.

These resources are especially valuable in secondary school collections.

An example of a statistical directory often used in library media centers is the *Statistical Abstract of the United States*, a basic source of statistical data on social and economic conditions in the United States as well as selected international data. *Statistical Abstract of the United States* is published annually and is available online (**www.census.gov/statab/www/**) and in both print (published by the Government Printing Office) and CD-ROM (published by the Bureau of the Census) formats.

The *Encyclopedia of Associations*, published five times a year by Gale Research, Inc., lists and describes over 23,000 associations and organizations. Broad subjects with detailed indexes divide this directory; a typical entry covers 15 to 20 basic points about the association or organization. The *Encyclopedia of Associations* is available in print format (three volumes), on CD-ROM (the equivalent of 13 print volumes), and online (**http://www.silverplatter.com/index.html**).

Almanacs. Where a single figure or fact is required, the almanac can be very useful. Students enjoy facts and trivia; almanacs are wonderful sources for browsing as well as information seeking. The *World Almanac and Book of Facts*, published annually by Funk and Wagnalls (1868 to present, print format), provides brief, accurate essays on topics of current interest. This almanac includes a quick reference index with approximately 75 broad subject headings; it also provides a section on maps and flags. The *World Almanac*, its CD-ROM equivalent, is published annually by Microsoft Corporation.

Information Please Almanac, published annually by Houghton Mifflin Co., is yet another popular almanac for school library media centers. *Information Please* (1974 to present) features discursive, larger units on such subjects as the lively arts, science, education, and medicine. The make-up of this almanac is considerably more attractive, with larger type and spacing than the *World Almanac*. The *Information Please Almanac* is also available online (**www.infoplease.com**), as is the *Information Please Kids Almanac* (**www.kids.infoplease.com**).

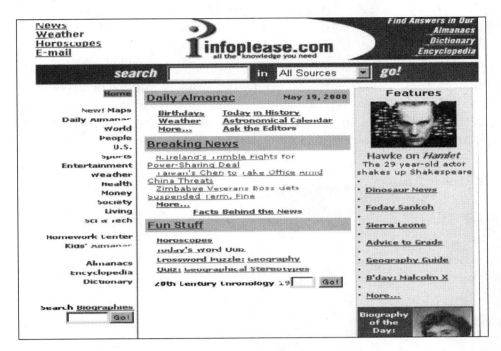

The *Daily Almanac* provides interesting facts about today's date. It includes categories such as Today's Figures, Today's Fun Facts, Today's Horoscope, Births, Deaths, and Special Events. The *Daily Almanac* is available online (**www.infoplease.com/cgi-bin/daily**).

Multitudes of specialized almanacs are available, many of them suitable for school library media centers. The following are examples of almanacs of a specific nature:

■ The *Almanac of American Politics* (National Journal) provides colorful profiles and insightful analyses of members of Congress as well as governors. Entries are arranged by state, name, and house committee. The almanac is easily searchable and updated frequently.

■ The *Living Almanac of Disasters* is an online resource (**www.disasterium.com**) that collects and explains disasters such as earthquakes and fires that happened on a particular day in history.

■ The *Writer's Almanac*, available online (**www.almanac.mpr.org**), can also be heard each day on public radio stations throughout the United States. This is a daily program of poetry and history offered by Garrison Keillor.

■ The *World Almanac of Presidential Quotations* (Pharos Book/St. Martin's Press), *The People's Almanac Presents Presidents of the Twentieth Century* (Little, Brown, & Co.), and *The World Almanac and Book of Facts 2000* (World Almanac) are examples of the numerous useful almanacs for secondary school library media centers.

■ *Information Please Environmental Almanac* (World Resources Institute) and *Almanac of the 50 States* (Information Publishing, 2000) are examples of almanacs particularly suitable for elementary school library media centers.

Let the knowledge of your school's specific needs, plus one or more of the many evaluation tools available, guide your media center's selection policies.

Yearbooks. Almost every imaginable area of human interest has its own yearbook. There are literally hundreds of yearbooks available. The following are four examples of yearbooks appropriate for school library media centers:

- *Facts on File* is a weekly digest of information covering political, social, cultural, and athletic events. Published by Facts on File, this print yearbook consists of weekly issues to be put in a yearly loose-leaf volume. The yearbook is also available on a CD-ROM containing the full text of "News Digest" from 1980 to present. *Facts on File* is also available online (**www.facts.com**).

- *Facts on File News Services* (or *Facts.com*) is an excellent fee-based online source (**www.2facts.com**) bringing together content from seven core reference databases to answer questions about events, issues, statistics, and people of the last 20 years. It includes 200 biographies, 130 key events, overviews of 50 controversial issues, and 500,000 hyperlinks. *Facts.com* is appropriate for middle and high school students; it introduces young adults to people and events that have shaped and are shaping our world. The cost is reasonable for school libraries, and the scope of content is very broad.

- The *Statesman's Yearbook*, published annually by St. Martin's Press, Inc., provides concise but complete descriptions of organizations and countries, emphasizing political and economic aspects of the world from 1864 to present.

■ The *American Book of Days*, published by H. W. Wilson and updated infrequently, discusses how and why holidays are celebrated. Beneath each day of the year, this yearbook lists major and minor events, many of which are explained in detailed essays.

Common types of yearbooks, not to be overlooked for school library media centers, are encyclopedia yearbooks, published with most major encyclopedias. Encyclopedia yearbooks identify names, dates, statistics, events, and other important items of the preceding year. These yearbooks, however, are being published less often, due to the increasing availability of electronic sources.

Handbooks. Handbooks zero in on specific areas of interest ranging from nature study to classical mythology. Look for handbooks of particular value to your community and student population. The *Guinness Book of Records*, published annually by Facts on File, is probably the most famous handbook. It was first published in 1956 and is divided into chapters pertaining to specific subjects, such as living world and human beings. This handbook is now available on CD-ROM titled *The Guinness Disc of Records*, published annually by Grolier Electronic Publishing. Specific *Guinness* titles address a variety of topics such as rock stars, names, and speed.

Famous First Facts, Fourth Edition, published by H. W. Wilson, is another popular handbook for school library media centers. *Famous First Facts* is just that—an alphabetical subject list of first happenings, discoveries, and inventions in American history.

Masterplots II, published by Salem Press in its Definitive Revised Edition (CD-ROM format), popular with secondary school students, provides plot summaries for over 2,000 books and abstracts of almost every important classic in the English language.

Monarch Notes (CD-ROM format published by the Bureau of Electronic Publishing), similar to *Masterplots II*, is useful for a summary of plot or content, character analysis, commentary on the text, and author background.

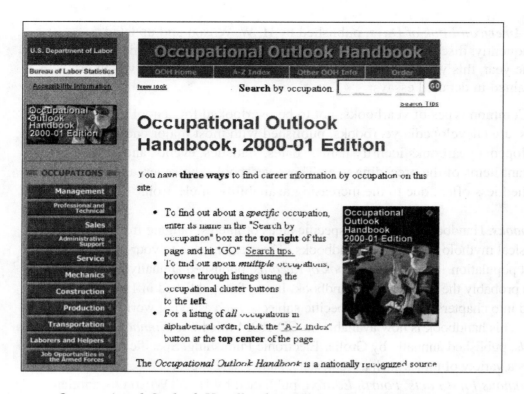

Occupational Outlook Handbook, published biennially by the U.S. Department of Labor and issued by the Government Printing Office, is also a favorite with secondary students. It provides detailed descriptions of more than 300 occupations covering 85 percent of all jobs in the United States. Each essay in the handbook indicates what a job is likely to offer in advancement, employment, location, earnings, and working conditions. The CD-ROM equivalent, titled *Occupational Outlook DISCovering Careers and Jobs*, is published annually by Gale Research, Inc. *Occupational Outlook Handbook* is also available online (**http://stats.bls.gov/ocohome.htm**).

Bartlett's Familiar Quotations, published by Little, Brown, and Co. (print format), is by far the most famous book of quotations. This handbook, including over 2,500 individuals and 20,000 quotations, is a collection of passages, phrases, and proverbs traced to their sources in ancient and modern times. *Bartlett's* can also be found online at **www.bartleby.com/99/index.html**.

Published by the Oxford University Press, *The Oxford Dictionary of Quotations* is also found in many school library media centers and contains more than 17,000 quotations; it is international in scope (see the following Web site for information: **www.oup.co.uk/reference/opr/quotations**).

An example of a current online quotation resource is Michael Moncur's *The Quotations Page* (**www.starlingtech.com/quotes**), a catalog of quotation resources on the Internet.

Handbooks, and the enormous range of topics they cover, are too numerous to treat individually, but the following examples illustrate the wide variety available for school library media centers today:

- *MLA Handbook for Writers of Research Papers* (Modern Language Association of America) and *Publication Manual of the American Psychological Association* (American Psychological Association);

- *Mayo Clinic Family Health Book* (print, William Morrow; CD-ROM, IVI Publishing);

- *Physicians' Desk Reference*, published annually by Medical Economics Data; CD-ROM published quarterly; available online (**www.pdr.net/gettingwell**);

- *The New Century Handbook of English Literature* (Appleton-Century Croft);

- *The American Inventors Instructional Handbook (*Dealco Manufacturing);

- *21st Century Grammar Handbook* (Dell Publishing Co.);

- *AIDS Crisis in America: A Reference Handbook* (ABC-CLIO);

- *2000 Handbook of United States Coins* (Golden Books Publishing Co.); and *101 Creative Problem-Solving Techniques: The Handbook of New Ideas for Business (*New Management Publishing Co.)

There are countless directories, almanacs, yearbooks, and handbooks. New ones, as well as old ones in new format, appear each year. It is obviously impossible to list all of them. In practice, library media specialists should select the ones that meet students' informational needs—and also mirror the unique qualities of the school, student population, and community served.

Chapter 5

Biographical Sources

Introduction

People are interesting; learning about individuals is fascinating. Students learn about people because they are curious and want to discover what others are like and have accomplished. What do biographical sources do? What is their purpose? Biographies tell about what people have done or are doing—their occupations, birth dates, major accomplishments, or their lives in general. Biographies are sources of fact as well as pictures of everyday life.

Types of Biographical Sources

There are two basic types of biographical sources: direct and indirect. Direct sources provide factual information about a person such as birth and death dates, place of birth, and career history. Well-known examples of direct sources are *Current Biography* and *Who's Who*. Indirect sources are typically indexes to other sources, bibliographic citations leading the student to other works that may contain the information sought. *Biography Index* is an example of an indirect source.

   These two types of biographical sources can be further divided into two categories: *current* and *retrospective*. Current sources provide information about living persons; retrospective sources supply information about historical figures. Some biographical tools give data on both living and dead individuals. Regardless of type or category, biographical sources vary in extent and coverage. Some sources, for example, focus on one profession or academic field, such as *American Presidents: Life Portraits*, which can be found online at (**www.americanpresidents.org**). Another class of biographies includes prominent figures from all fields who live in a specific geographic location, such as *Who's Who in the East* [America] (Marquis Who's Who/Reed Reference Publishing).

   Biographical sources can also be international in scope. *Lives and Legacies*

Series: An Encyclopedia of People Who Changed the World is an example of an online international biographical source that links the achievements of the past to developments of the present (**www.oryxpress.com**).

Since interest in the lives of others is universal, biographical sources are an essential and significant reference tool for school library media specialists.

Evaluation and Selection

As with all other reference sources for school library media centers, selection of appropriate biographical items must be based on the needs of the school, students, and community, which will vary widely according to age level, location of school, and other variables. Students require biographies for research purposes and general information needs, as well as to satisfy their personal curiosities. Both current and retrospective biographical sources are essential tools in library media centers.

An overriding factor regarding selection of biographical sources is cost. As a library media specialist, you must consider the importance of purchasing full-volume sets or a concise one-volume source. You must also decide which format will give you the most for your money. Should the biographical source be print, a

Evaluation of Biographical Sources

COST
- Determine the most useful format you can afford.
- Consider one-volume sources as opposed to full-volume sets.
- Always consider the needs of the school and student population.

ACCURACY
- Primary sources are written by the subject; secondary sources are written by other individuals.
- Primary sources may omit information the author does not want to divulge.
- Secondary sources may be incorrect or biased.

COMPREHENSIVENESS
- Criteria for inclusion are typically explained in the prefatory material.
- How the criteria are defined and applied determines the comprehensiveness of the source.
- The scope and criteria should be in agreement.

EASE OF USE
- The source should be concise, organized, and straightforward.
- Indexes and cross-references should be included.
- Electronic sources have advantages due to ease of searching.

CURRENCY
- Compare resource with similar works to determine if it is up to date.
- Check publication frequency.

CD-ROM, or purchased as an online resource? The answer will depend on budget and student needs. Does your library media center have the hardware to warrant the purchase of CD-ROMs and online services? Are the students capable of efficiently and effectively searching electronically?

Many biographical sources are available in several formats. *American Men and Women of Science*, for instance, is offered in print format (eight volumes), on CD-ROM (titled *New Scientist*, published quarterly), and online at (**www.bowker.com/catalog/**). Some sources remain available in print format only, although this is changing rapidly. Searching is typically more thorough in an electronic format than in a print source. In addition, one is able to scan thousands of possibilities in seconds, rather than laboriously searching through individual indexes and sources. Electronic sources can also include video clips, links to other Web sites, and additional aids. Your school, students, community, cost, and character of your library media center will all play a role in the effective selection of biographical sources.

How does a library media specialist know if a biographical source, print or electronic, is legitimate and accurate? As with other reference tools, biographical sources should be evaluated as to their accuracy, comprehensiveness, and ease of use. For current resources, the information must be as up-to-date as possible.

Of critical importance in evaluating a biographical source is the *accuracy* of the information provided. There are two sources of this information: the subjects themselves and the information given about them (secondary sources). While biographers' subjects or authors of autobiographies are certainly capable of providing accurate information, they may omit facts that they regard as unfavorable. Retrospective biographers must rely on secondary sources for their information. These sources may have incorrect or biased information, depending on their authors. It is always best to consult other sources if you question the facts.

Typically, the criteria for inclusion in a specific biographical source are provided in prefatory material, but how those criteria are defined and applied determines how *comprehensive* the source is. The higher the number of individuals meeting those criteria who are included in the source, the more valuable it is. Often the criteria are stated in such general terms that inclusiveness is difficult to determine. Regardless of the criteria used, the source's scope should conform to them.

As with all reference tools, *ease of use* is a critical factor. If the source is poorly organized, or if the indexes or cross-references are inadequate, one may never locate the information desired. Obviously, electronic sources offer a definite advantage over print materials concerning ease of use. Electronic retrieval (CD-ROM, online) allows students to retrieve biographical entries for individuals with common characteristics (date of birth, occupation). Electronic searching also permits students to simultaneously search entries from different printed editions or volumes of a specific biographical tool. Information, regardless of format, should be presented in a concise, organized, straightforward fashion.

Currency is also important in evaluating biographical sources. Out-of-date information can lead to inaccuracies in the subject's address, current profession, or other specific. Comparing entries for the same person in varying biographical sources may reveal errors. Publication frequency is another issue in maintaining current information. Biographical directories are typically revised every year or two. However, the electronic versions of these sources are often updated only when a new print edition is prepared and therefore may be no more current than the print sources. Biographical dictionaries are revised less frequently. However, dictionaries that are published serially, such as *Current Biography,* often publish new or revised entries on prominent people whose earlier entries are out-of-date.

Fortunately, the library media specialist has tools and aids to help in evaluation and selection of biographical sources. Many of the review journals described in Chapter 2 contain separate sections regarding reference works. Use these tools to identify the most suitable biographical sources for your school. Also enlist the assistance of other faculty members who are experts in the field.

Basic Sources

Numerous biographical reference sources are available on every imaginable "significant person" and in every format. The focus of this section, however, is biographical sources appropriate for use in school library media centers. Your choices will depend on your situation—the school, students, and community, as well as budget and personal preferences. The biographical sources mentioned here are commonly used; they are not all-inclusive, but merely examples suitable for school library media centers. Further information about specific biographical sources is presented in journals and other evaluation and selection tools (as explained in Chapter 2).

Who's Whos. *Who's Who in America* (print format), a three-volume set by Marquis Who's Who/Reed Reference Publishing, is a current biographical *directory* useful for many school library media centers. Published biennially and arranged alphabetically, it includes individuals based on their achievements and contributions to society, not their wealth or notoriety. The information is obtained firsthand from the subject, if possible. *Who's Who in America* is primarily used to locate basic information about individuals such as date of birth, positions held, address, and degrees earned. This source is usually the first source to consult when a student requests basic biographical data on a prominent American.

Who's Who publishes four United States regional directories: East, Midwest, West, and South/Southwest (Marquis Who's Who/Reed Reference Publishing). Canada and Mexico are included in each regional *Who's Who.* Several topical *Who's Whos* are also published on topics such as entertainment and religion. Examples of others are *Who's Who Among Black Americans* (Gale Research Publishing), *Who's Who in Media and Communications* (Marquis Who's Who/Reed Reference Publishing), *Who's Who Among Hispanic Americans* (Gale Research Publishing), *Who's Who in American Art* (print format published biennially), and *Who's Who in American Politics* (print format published every two years) by Marquis Who's Who; the last two can also be found online at (**www.marquiswhoswho.com/products/whosol.html**).

Who's Who is also international in scope. Two examples are *Who's Who in the World,* published every two years by Marquis Who's Who/Reed Reference Publishing, and *The International Who's Who,* published annually by Gibralter Publishing Company.

Current Biographical Dictionaries. *Current Biography* (H.W. Wilson, print format published monthly except December; CD-ROM published annually; online at **www.hwwilson.com/databases/cbcdrom.htm**), is one of the most recognized current biographical *dictionaries. Current Biography* provides objective and carefully researched biographical essays about persons in a wide range of fields; persons prominent in their disciplines. The essays are primarily based on articles that have appeared in newspapers and magazines. Each essay includes a photograph of the biographee and a list of sources upon which the essay is based. It provides a life history of the individual without reading a full biography. Each issue of *Current Biography* contains approximately 15 essays; at the end of each year, the essays from the monthly issues are collated in the *Current Biography Yearbook*.

A widely used biographical source for middle and high schools is *Biography Today*, published by Omnigraphics in three softbound issues and one bound, cumulative annual volume. Each issue contains entries for 15 to 20 persons judged to be of interest to young people.

An extremely valuable online biographical source is **www.biography.com**, which offers 25,000 personalities and 2,500 videos for the user to search. Biography.com also features "Born on This Day," "Top 10 Biographies," "Biographies on Arts and Entertainment," "Features," "Biography Book Club" and numerous other useful biographical elements.

Author Sources and Literary Criticism

One significant area in many school media reference collections is author sources. Students study and learn about the lives of authors as a part of the curriculum. The library media center can supplement these studies with visiting authors and similar activities. The following are examples of author sources appropriate for school library media centers:

■ *Contemporary Authors*, published by Gale Research Publishing (print format is updated annually; CD-ROM semiannually), is a current biographical dictionary that includes not only authors of books, but journalists, musicians, and others.

■ A similar biographical source is *Something About the Author* (Gale Research Publishing). Several volumes are published each year and each volume contains a cumulative index to the entire set, which includes authors and illustrators of works for children and young adults.

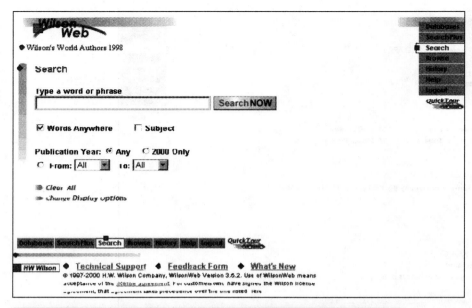

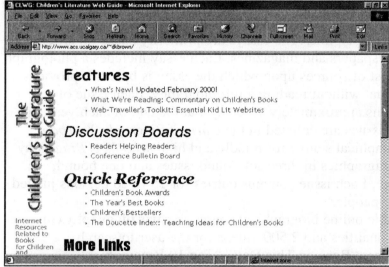

■ *World Authors* (H.W. Wilson, updated periodically) is yet another well-known series on authors. This international source includes not only essential biographical information but also bibliographies of works by and about the author. Entries are from 800 to 1,600 words, with a picture of the author and a list of published works.

Examples of the numerous online sources about authors and literary criticism are *The Reference Center at the Internet Public Library* (**www.ipl.org/ref**) and *The Children's Literature Web Guide* (**www.acs.ucalgary.ca/~dkbrown**). These two resources offer excellent author information as well as sections on literary criticism. Also useful for school library media centers are:

■ *Booktalk* (**www.booktalk.com**),

■ *Author Biographies* (**www.myunicorn.com/biblios.html**),

■ *Authors* (**http://authors.miningco.com/**),

■ *The Literary Menagerie,* (**http://sunset.backbone.olemiss.edu/~egcash/**), and

■ *Gale Literary Index* (**www.galenet.com/servlet/LitIndex**).

Native American Author Sources

ELECTRONIC RESOURCES

- *Native American Authors* (**www.ipl.org/ref/native/biblio2.html**)
- *The North American Native Authors Catalog* (**www.nativeauthors.com/**)
- *Native American Books* (**http://indy4.fdl.cc.mn.us/~isk/books/bookmenu.html**)
- *Index of Native American Resources on the Internet* (**http://hanksville.phast.umass.edu/misc/Naresources.html**)
- *Indigenous Peoples' Literature* (**www.indians.org/natlit.htm**)

PRINT RESOURCES

- *American Indian Autobiography* (University of California Press)
- *American Indian Literature: An Anthology* (University of Oklahoma Press)
- *A Bibliography of Native American Writers 1772-1924* (Scarecrow Press)
- *Biographical Dictionary of Indians of the Americas* (American Indian Publishing, Inc.)
- *Blue Dawn, Red Earth: New Native American Storytellers* (Doubleday)
- *Dictionary of Native American Literature* (Garland Publishing, Inc.)
- *Harper's Anthology of 20th Century Native American Poetry* (Harper & Row)
- *Home Places: Contemporary Native American Writings* (University of Arizona Press)
- *Literature by and About the American Indian: An Annotated Bibliography* (Illinois National Council of Teachers of English)
- *Literature of the American Indian: Views and Interpretations. A Gathering of Indian Memories, Symbolic Contexts and Literary Criticism* (New American Libraries)
- *Native American Literature* (Twayne Publishers)
- *Native American Literature: A Brief Introduction and Anthology* (HarperCollins College Publishers)
- *Native American Women: A Biographical Dictionary* (Garland Publishing)
- *Native Americans Autobiography: An Anthology* (University of Wisconsin Press)
- *Native Americans: Portrait of the Peoples* (Visible Ink Press)
- *Returning the Gift: Poetry and Prose from the First North American Native Writers Festival* (University of Arizona Press)
- *Who Was When in Native American History: Indians and Non-Indians from Early Contacts Through 1900* (Facts on File)

African Author Sources

- *African Authors: A Companion to Black African Writing*
  By Donald E. Herdeck, Washington: Inscape Corporation
- *African American Literature: A Brief Introduction and Anthology*
  Al Young, compiler, NY: HarperCollins College Publishers
- *A Bibliographical Guide to African-American Women Writers*
  Casper LeRoy Jordan, compiler, Westport, Connecticut: Greenwood Press
- *Bibliography of African Literature*
  Peter Limb and Jean-Marie Volet, Lanham, Maryland: Scarecrow Press
- *Binding Cultures: Black Women Writers in Africa and the Diaspora*
  By Gay Wilentz, Bloomington: Indiana University Press
- *Modern African American Writers*
  Matthew J. Bruccoli and Judith S. Baughman, series editors, New York:
  Facts on File
- *Who's Who in African Literature: Biographies, Works, Commentaries*
  Commentaries by Janheinz Jahn, Ulla Schild, and Almut Nordmann, Erdmann
  H. Jubingen

Hispanic Author Sources

- *Biographical Dictionary of Hispanic Literature in the United States: The Literature of the Puerto Ricans, Cuban Americans, and Other Hispanic Writers.* New York: Greenwood Press
- *Borinquen: An Anthology of Puerto Rican Literature.* New York: Alfred Knopf
- *Contemporary Spanish.* Westport, Connecticut: Greenwood Press
- *Dictionary of Hispanic Biography.* New York: Gale Research
- *Dictionary of Twentieth Century Cuban Literature.* New York: Greenwood Press
- *Iguana Dreams: New Latino Fiction.* New York: Harper Perennial
- *Inventing A Word: An Anthology of Twentieth Century Puerto Rican Poetry.* New York: Columbia University Press
- *Latino Materials: A Multimedia Guide for Children and Young Adults.* Chicago: American Library Association
- *Spanish-American Literature: A History* (Volumes 1 and 2). 2nd edition. Detroit, Michigan: Wayne State University Press

Retrospective Biographical Dictionaries, unlike current dictionaries, deal with people who are no longer living. A major biographical source of this type for school library media centers is the *McGraw-Hill Encyclopedia of World Biography* (McGraw-Hill), compiled specifically for students in secondary schools. Subjects are selected with curriculum needs in mind. Inclusion is by conventional standards of importance or familiarity, though living persons are occasionally included. This reference work consists of 11 volumes of text and a twelfth volume containing index and study guides. Each entry is written by an authority who knows the subject personally; portraits are included. By means of the study guides in Volume 12, one may develop a list of individuals associated with significant events, eras, or historical trends. The biographical essays guide students to further sources of information. Dates and facts tend to be reliable because authors are selected for their expertise in the field.

For ready-reference purposes *Webster's New Biographical Dictionary* (G & C Merriam Company) offers brief information but more comprehensive coverage—one-paragraph descriptions of the important contributions of approximately 30,000 individuals from the past.

The *Dictionary of American Biography* (Charles Scribner's Sons) is an excellent source for extensive biographical information about prominent deceased Americans. Its more than 18,000 entries are arranged alphabetically by surname. Written by scholars, they are entirely in essay format and vary from a couple of paragraphs to several pages (a few as long as 10 pages).

The Concise Dictionary of American Biography (Charles Scribner's Sons) is a one-volume work of brief entries; some offer only basic facts, while more important figures have short essays.

Another important retrospective source is *Who Was Who in America* (Marquis Who's Who/Reed Reference Publishing), which provides basic factual data about deceased prominent Americans; it is revised every four to five years.

Indirect biographical sources tell where information about individuals may be found rather than providing the information directly. An indirect source is the best place to start a search for information about a person if the student requests a number of different sources. *Biography Index* offers references to biographical articles in nearly 3,000 periodicals and to nearly 2,000 book-length individual and collective biographies. It is available in print format, CD-ROM and online at (**www.hwwilson.com/databases/bioind.htm**). The print format is published quarterly with cumulative annual and biennial volumes; the CD-ROM format is revised quarterly, and the online version is updated twice a week.

Conclusion

Library media specialists have a massive number of biographical sources from which to choose. The purpose of this chapter is to introduce you to types of biographical sources and to provide useful examples within each type. Each school library media center's selections will depend on its own situation. Not only is there a wide variety of biographical sources, both individual and collective, to choose from, but resources now come in a selection of formats as well. Biographical information can also be found in other reference sources such as encyclopedias. Each library media specialist's search strategy employed will depend on the type and amount of biographical information students ask for. As with most reference questions, the first step is to obtain as much information as possible from the student. Can the question be answered by searching one source (ready-reference) or will it require a variety of sources (research)? Regardless of the question, you can answer it only if you have the proper biographical sources in your school library media center.

Chapter 6

Dictionaries and Encyclopedias

Dictionaries indicate spelling, meaning, pronunciation, and syllabication of words. General encyclopedias capsulize and organize the world's accumulated knowledge. This chapter discusses types of dictionaries and encyclopedias appropriate for school library media centers, as well as evaluation and selection of these reference sources.

DICTIONARIES

Introduction

Dictionaries are primarily thought of as a means of verifying spelling and defining words. However, these reference sources cover almost every imaginable interest. Dictionaries are of two basic types: Reference books containing words usually arranged along with information about their forms, pronunciations, functions, etymologies, meanings, and syntactical and idiomatic uses; and reference books alphabetically listing terms or names important to a particular subject or activity, along with discussion of their meanings and applications.

Dictionaries may either be descriptive (how the language is actually used) or prescriptive (how it ought to be used). The descriptive philosophy claims that language is ever changing and that dictionaries should reflect those changes. Believers in the descriptive viewpoint realize that few rules are absolute; different societal and cultural situations demand their own rules. The prescriptive view claims that the major role of dictionaries is to set standards, support traditional usage, and prevent corruption of language by jargon and slang. Most of the Merriam-Webster dictionaries take the stance that "almost anything goes" as long as it is popular. At the other end of the spectrum are dictionaries that provide absolute rules of usage, such as *Webster's New World Dictionary*. Somewhere in between descriptive and prescriptive dictionaries are the more practical types, such as *The American Heritage Dictionary*.

Two additional categories of dictionaries are *unabridged* and *abridged*. An unabridged dictionary attempts to include all of the words in the language in use at the time the dictionary is assembled. Unabridged dictionaries may contain over 265,000 words. Abridged dictionaries are selectively compiled and typically based on a larger dictionary. They are created for a certain level of student use and contain between 130,000 and 265,000 words. Most dictionaries are abridged. Types of dictionaries other than English language include foreign language, historical, slang and dialect, thesauri, subject, and visual.

Visual Dictionaries

- *What's What, A Visual Glossary of the Physical World* (Smithmark)
- *The Perigee Visual Dictionary of Signing: An A to Z Guide to Over 1,250 Signs of American Sign Language* (Perigree Books)
- *The Visual Dictionary of Chemistry* (Dorling Kindersley)
- *The Facts on File English/Spanish Visual Dictionary* (Facts on File)
- *The American Heritage Picture Dictionary* (Houghton Mifflin)
- *Children's Dictionary of Occupations* (Career Futures, Inc.)
- *The Macmillan Visual Dictionary* (Macmillan)
- *The Oxford Picture Word Book* (Oxford University Press)
- *The Picture Dictionary* (National Library Publications)
- *Ultimate Visual Dictionary* (Dorling Kindersley)
- *The Visual Dictionary of Ancient Civilizations* (Dorling Kindersley)
- *The Visual Dictionary of Dinosaurs* (Dorling Kindersley)
- *The Visual Dictionary of Plants* (Dorling Kindersley)
- *The Visual Dictionary of the Earth* (Dorling Kindersley)
- *The Visual Dictionary of the Universe* (Dorling Kindersley)

Evaluation and Selection

Remember, above all else, that no dictionary is perfect; language is continually evolving. Each dictionary has its good features and its defects. Basically, dictionaries are written for a specific audience, such as high school students, or for a particular purpose. In evaluating dictionaries, it is critical to determine how well a dictionary fulfills the purpose or meets the needs of the population addressed. These are exceptionally critical elements for school library media specialists who serve unique populations. Authority, format, currency, and accuracy should be considered in evaluating dictionaries for school library media centers.

The *authority* or reputation of the publisher is an essential factor in judging the quality of dictionaries, as staffs, rather than individuals, normally compile them. Look for reputable publishers. The larger, better-known publishers in North America include Merriam-Webster; Random House; Scott Foresman; Houghton Mifflin; Macmillan; Simon and Schuster; and Oxford University Press. There are additional reputable publishers for specialized dictionaries.

Major *format* considerations for dictionaries include binding, arrangement of words, and readability. School library media centers should have at least one comprehensive, hardcover dictionary that will withstand frequent use. Readability is a particularly important consideration for library media centers. Is the print size large enough? Is boldface type used effectively? Is it clear and user-friendly? Dictionaries should be judged on how well they achieve the purpose stated in the title or introduction. For example, an elementary-level dictionary should include words likely to be used in writing by an elementary student.

The major advantages of dictionaries in electronic format are multiple access points and time saved by searching. When a dictionary is available electronically, the library media specialist should ask all of the usual questions regarding its value relative to the printed version.

Currency is yet another important factor to consider. Dictionary revision is never-ending. New words, revised definitions of older words with new meanings, deletions and additions of technical terms are continually occurring. An obvious

---

Evaluation of Dictionaries

AUTHORITY
- A reputable publisher is important. Some reputable publishers are:
- Merriam-Webster
- Random House
- Scott Foresman
- Houghton Mifflin
- Macmillan
- Simon & Schuster
- Oxford University Press

FORMAT
- Consider binding, arrangement of words, and readability.
- Note whether the dictionary achieves the purpose set forth in the title or introduction.
- Electronic dictionaries have the advantages of multiple access points and quicker searching.

CURRENCY
- Because dictionary revision is never-ending, this is an important consideration when evaluating dictionaries.
- Due to the fact that a major advantage of electronic dictionaries is rapid update, use of this information during the evaluation process is critical.

ACCURACY
- Spelling and definition should be precise.
- Words should be "modernized."
- Meanings should be precise and clearly indicated.
- Definitions should be understandable and unambiguous.
- Illustrative examples and quotations from literature are helpful.

advantage of electronic dictionaries is rapid updates. Be aware, however, that just because a dictionary is electronic does not necessarily mean that it is more current than the print equivalent.

In determining the *accuracy* of dictionaries, two major considerations are spelling and definition. Where there are several forms of spelling, they should be clearly indicated. Frequently, two different spellings are provided and both are acceptable. One should check words that have been "modernized." Dictionaries usually give the modern meaning of words first. Meanings should be precise; separate and distinct meanings of words should be indicated clearly. Definitions should reflect the meanings of words in understandable, unambiguous terms. Illustrative examples or quotations from literature can assist in defining words in context.

The *selection* of dictionaries, as well as other reference materials, should be based on the particular needs and requirements of the school, student population, and community served. Additional elements to consider are budget and age and condition of the dictionaries currently in the library media center collection. The long, useful life of a large and comprehensive dictionary will typically justify the cost. Remain alert to dictionaries geared specifically to school library media centers and the fact that college-level dictionaries might be valuable in high school library media centers, particularly for advanced students.

When you select dictionaries, read reviews and stick with standard titles. Use selection tools such as *Kister's Best Dictionaries for Adults and Young People: A Comparative Guide* (Oryx Press) and reviews provided in *Booklist* (American Library Association) journal.

Basic Sources

English Language Dictionaries. Probably the most notable *unabridged* dictionary of the English language is *Webster's Third New International* (Merriam-Webster, Inc.). (Something to note: there is no copyright on the use of the word "Webster." It is common property; anyone may use it.) This large, comprehensive dictionary includes such items as the date when a word or phrase first entered the language and identification of vocabulary specifically of American origin. Random House offers an unabridged dictionary in CD-ROM format, titled the *Random House Unabridged Electronic Dictionary*. This current, descriptive-style dictionary includes 315,000 entries and 2,500 illustrations.

There are numerous *abridged* dictionaries appropriate for school library media centers. *Merriam-Webster's Collegiate Dictionary* (print format) represents an extensive revision and updating in both the entries and special sections. Each entry includes the part of speech, pronunciation, inflections, etymology, definitions, and notes on usage and synonymy. Definitions in this dictionary are precise and clear.

Another useful abridged dictionary in print format is *The Concise American Heritage Dictionary,* which is the abridged version of *The American Heritage Dictionary of the English Language* (Houghton Mifflin). This dictionary is particularly appropriate for high school students. It is easy to read and the typeface and illustrations are large and clear. *The Concise American Heritage Dictionary* is extremely complete for a condensed edition. Other suitable abridged dictionaries in print format are *Webster's New World Dictionary of the American Language* (Prentice-Hall) and *The Random House Webster's College Dictionary* (Random House).

For elementary age students, the following abridged dictionaries in print format are appropriate:

■ *American Heritage First Dictionary* (Houghton Mifflin),

■ *Macmillan First Dictionary* (Simon & Schuster),

■ *Scott Foresman Beginning Dictionary* (Scott Foresman),

■ *Webster's Elementary Dictionary* (Merriam-Webster),

■ *Thorndike-Barnhart Children's Dictionary* (Scott Foresman),

■ *Longman Elementary Dictionary* (Addison Wesley Longman), and

■ *American Heritage Children's Dictionary* (Houghton Mifflin).

Several abridged dictionaries in CD-ROM format are currently available and valuable in library media center collections. *Random House Webster's Dictionary and Thesaurus College Edition* (Random House) and *The American Heritage Talking Dictionary* (Houghton Mifflin) are reputable electronic dictionaries; they vary slightly in arrangement, format, and length of definitions. For elementary school students, *The World Book Dictionary* and *Macmillan Dictionary for Children* (both CD-ROM format) are reliable choices.

An excellent online source is *The New Encarta World English Dictionary* by Microsoft Corporation (**http://www.worldenglishdictionary.com/**), which claims to be the first newly written English dictionary in 30 years. *Encarta* includes hundreds of new words and a focus on how English is spoken around the world. It also contains a complete thesaurus, book of quotations, style guide, and almanac. Another reputable online dictionary is *Dictionary.com* (**www.dictionary.com**), a valuable general English language dictionary for school library media centers.

Great Dictionaries for Children

PRINT FORMAT
■ *American Heritage Children's Dictionary* (Houghton Mifflin)
■ *American Heritage First Dictionary* (American Heritage)
■ *The Children's Visual Dictionary* (Dorling Kindersley)
■ *Longman Elementary Dictionary* (Addison Wesley Longman)
■ *Macmillan First Dictionary* (Simon & Schuster)
■ *My Big Dictionary* (Houghton Mifflin)
■ *My First Dictionary* (Scott Foresman)
■ *My First Picture Dictionary* (Scott Foresman)
■ *Picture Dictionary: English* (Houghton Mifflin)
■ *Scott Foresman Beginning Dictionary* (Scott Foresman)
■ *Thorndike-Barnhart Children's Dictionary* (Scott Foresman)
■ *Thorndike-Barnhart Junior Dictionary* (Addison Wesley)
■ *Webster's Elementary Dictionary* (Merriam-Webster)
■ *Webster's II Children's Dictionary* (Houghton Mifflin)
■ *Webster's New World Children's Dictionary* (IDG Books Worldwide)

Foreign Language Dictionaries. A student who simply seeks a common foreign word or phrase is likely to find the answer in almost any general dictionary. However, when it comes to more complicated, specialized words, students should refer to a bilingual dictionary. There are several reputable publishers of foreign language dictionaries: Cassell, HarperCollins, Charles Scribner's Sons, Simon and Schuster, and Oxford University Press. Their dictionaries all provide similar information, including pronunciations, definitions, slang words, colloquialisms, and idioms. Foreign language dictionaries are essential resources for school library media centers. The types and number of foreign language dictionaries purchased will, of course, depend on the school's curriculum and student body.

Historical Dictionaries. *The Oxford English Dictionary* (Oxford University Press, print and CD-ROM formats) is a scholarly compilation including extensive etymologies that record the history of words and meanings in use since 1150. The purpose of this dictionary is to trace the history of the English language. *The Oxford English Dictionary* in CD-ROM format is considerably less expensive than the print version. *The New Shorter Oxford English Dictionary* (print format) is a current, two-volume historical dictionary that includes over 500,000 words and 83,000 quotations. *The New Shorter* is moderately priced and an excellent resource for learning etymologies and fine points of history. The single volume, *Barnhart Dictionary of Etymology* (H. W. Wilson) is yet another historical dictionary. An excellent feature of this dictionary is that it emphasizes the way language is written and spoken in the United States today.

Slang and Dialect Dictionaries. Does a library media center need dictionaries on slang and dialect? This question is debatable and depends on the particular school and community served. However, slang and dialect dictionaries are useful for indicating the variations of meanings of slang words as well as providing expressions that are not well defined in an ordinary dictionary. The most notable slang and dialect dictionaries include *The Oxford Dictionary of Modern Slang* (Oxford University Press)*; The Thesaurus of Slang* (Facts on File)*; Random House Historical Dictionary of American Slang and Dictionary of American Regional English* (Harvard University Press). An example of an online slang dictionary is *A Dictionary of Slang* (www.peevish.co.uk/slang).

Thesauri are specialized dictionaries that deal solely with word synonyms and antonyms. The best known thesauri are the work of Peter Mark Roget. (Like "Webster's," "Roget's" cannot be copyrighted and is free to any publisher.) The most notable Roget's thesaurus is the *Roget's International Thesaurus* (HarperCollins, print format). Two additional Roget's in print format that are valuable for library media center collections are *Roget's A to Z* and *Roget's II: The New Thesaurus* (HarperCollins).

Thesauri are also available on CD-ROM (as well as online via word processing). Two thesauri in CD-ROM format include *Roget's II: Electronic Thesaurus* (Houghton Mifflin) and *Merriam-Webster's Collegiate Thesaurus* (Merriam-Webster). Both contain over 75,000 entries and have the advantage of rapid, easy searching. Random House also offers a combination of thesaurus and dictionary in CD-ROM format, *Random House Webster's Dictionary and Thesaurus College Edition.*

Examples of Subject Dictionaries

- *A Dictionary of Battles* (Wordsworth Editions, Inc.)
- *Dictionary of Classical Mythology* (Cassell Academic)
- *Harvard Dictionary of Music* (Belknap Press)
- *A Dictionary of Media Terms* (Fitzroy Dearborn Publishing)
- *Dictionary of Geography* (Oxford University Press)
- *Dictionary of Science and Technology* (Academic Press)
- *A Consumer's Dictionary of Food Additives* (Three Rivers Press)
- *Dictionary of Fictional Characters* (Writers Publishing)
- *Concise Dictionary of the Opera* (Oxford University Press)
- *The Civil War Dictionary* (Vintage Books, Random House)
- *The New Dictionary of American Family Names* (New American Library)
- *The Illustrated Computer Dictionary for Dummies* (IDG Books Worldwide)
- *A Basic Dictionary of ASL* (American Sign Language) *Terms* (online)
  http://www.masterstech-home.com/ASLDict.html

Subject Dictionaries explain meanings of specific words in terms of professions, occupations, or areas of interest. When selecting subject dictionaries, the library media specialist must determine that no other resource currently in the collection provides the same or remarkably similar information. It is important to look for purposeful illustrations, clear and thorough definitions, and current terminology in subject dictionaries.

There is an enormity of subject dictionaries available dealing with every imaginable area of interest. The above resources are examples of the wide variety of subject dictionaries available in print format that are appropriate for school library media centers.

With dictionaries now available on most word processing software, the focus of general dictionaries has altered. Many features common to general dictionaries are provided online (spelling, synonyms), providing easy and rapid access to basic dictionary functions. However, dictionaries provide much more than the basic word processing features. In addition, a dictionary is often required when one is not working at a computer. There still remains a distinct place for print versions of general, foreign language, historical, slang and dialect, thesauri, and subject dictionaries in even the most technological school library media centers.

ENCYCLOPEDIAS

Introduction

Encyclopedias have traveled remarkable distances over the past few decades with the expansion of new technologies. In all formats, encyclopedias are essential reference sources for school library media centers. A majority of ready-reference, as well as research questions (to a degree), can be answered using encyclopedias. The literal definition of "encyclopedia" is a work that contains information on all branches of knowledge or comprehensively treats a particular aspect of knowledge, usually via articles arranged alphabetically by subject. The purposes of encyclopedias are to educate and inform.

These reference sources are unique in that they are organized and packaged in such a way that information is easily accessible and retrievable. Encyclopedias gather information from a variety of fields or from a single subject area and arrange it for rapid answers. Through detailed articles and brief facts, encyclopedias make an effort to include a wide range of information from a multitude of topics. Note, however, that there are limits to the breadth and depth of information contained in encyclopedias. These resources are useful for ready-reference, factual questions "Where is Dubai?"; for background information "How is oil refined?"; and for pre-research teaching of systematic approaches to information-gathering.

Encyclopedias should not be considered as sole sources of information, although they do assist in directing and strengthening students' subsequent work. Encyclopedias are among the most frequently used reference materials in school library media centers. Differences in quality (for instance, between *Compton's* and *World Book*) are subtle but significant.

In addition to the traditional multi-volume general encyclopedias, there are two other important types for school library media centers: single-volume and subject encyclopedias. Encyclopedias can also be divided into three general categories: format (general, single volume, and subject); scope (general and subject); and audience (children, young adult, and layperson). Remain aware that encyclopedias are not proper resources for involved research; they are merely springboards to further information.

Evaluation and Selection

Evaluating a large multi-volume set of encyclopedias is a complicated procedure. It is rare to find errors of commission in encyclopedia sets, since editorial standards are high in encyclopedia publishing. However, with some sets there are serious problems with updating. Outdated material persists, not because the editorial staff is unaware of changes that should be made, but because their budget allows them to update only a certain number of pages each year. The cost of writing new copy is not the problem; indeed, some encyclopedias have updated articles in the CD-ROM version that are not in the print set. It is production costs—setting type, making film, stripping in art or text—that limit the amount of revision in a print set. Remember, however, that an encyclopedia is not supposed to take the place of a newspaper in reporting current events. Also evaluate encyclopedia bibliographies, looking at the publication dates of materials listed and remembering that age in some subject areas is not necessarily a flaw.

In evaluating CD-ROMs it is more difficult to find what is new to a release. Publishers of CD-ROM encyclopedias continue to follow different marketing strategies, which accounts in part for disparities in price. *Collier's, Compton's,* and *Encarta* are available at retail as well as for the school and library market. *Encyclopedia Americana* on CD-ROM, on the other hand, is sold only to schools and libraries. All of them provide updates that can be downloaded from the Internet, in some cases for a subscription fee. CD-ROMs have been thought of as a

---

Evaluation of Encyclopedias

ACCURACY
- Compare for accuracy. It cannot be assumed.
- Look for standard titles.
- Consult appropriate review sources.

AUTHORITY
- Consider the reputations of the writers, contributor, editors, and publisher.
- Look for prominent contributors.
- Stick with reputable publishing companies.

CURRENCY
- Remember that "Edition" does not indicate currency.

FORMAT
- Illustrations should be current, functional, clear, easy to follow, and appropriate for the intended audience.
- Motion and sound (electronic format) should be functional, clear, and suitable for the audience.
- The source should be user-friendly.
- The format should advance the purpose.

INDEXING
- A detailed index is an absolute necessity.

OBJECTIVITY
- Check for objectivity. Do not assume all encyclopedias are objective.
- Check for subtle or implicit biases.
- Notice what is excluded, emphasized, or trivialized.

SCOPE
- The scope should be appropriate for the age group it claims to serve.
- The subject coverage should be uniform from discipline to discipline.
- Contemporary issues should be included.

transitional technology, and now, with the dramatic growth of the Web, it is easier to see where the future might lie. However, it is too early to count CD-ROMs out. Electronic encyclopedias provide a good case-in-point of the strengths and weaknesses of both formats. CD-ROMs cannot be updated as frequently as online, but are still the best way to provide all the "bells and whistles." The encyclopedias that combine the multimedia capabilities of CD-ROMs with updating and Web links available through the Internet offer the best of both worlds.

Like dictionaries, encyclopedias are typically published with a particular audience in mind. Accuracy, authority, currency, format, indexing, objectivity, and scope are the criteria to keep in mind when *evaluating* encyclopedias for school library media center use.

Accuracy and reliability of encyclopedias cannot be assumed. Like all other reference sources, they are written by individuals and therefore may contain errors. For evaluation purposes, one should look for standard titles and consult appropriate review sources.

The *authority* of encyclopedias can be determined by the reputations of the scholars who write (or sign) individual articles (or who are listed as contributors) and the publisher who distributes the encyclopedia. An editorial staff refines the work, so even the scholars are constrained by editorial parameters. In evaluating encyclopedias, one should look for prominent contributors, leaders in their fields, and ask how their qualifications relate to the articles they wrote. It is also advisable to stick with reputable publishing companies.

Currency of encyclopedias is not as critical a factor with regard to evaluation as it was in the past. Technologies have made the process of revising and updating considerably easier. Most large publishers claim to revise approximately 10 percent of their material each year. This claim to ongoing revision is a major selling point, as publishers believe that no library media center will purchase a new encyclopedia unless there have been major revisions and updates. Often the text will be revised while the bibliography remains dated. Be aware that the use of the word "edition" does not indicate currency. A printing of an encyclopedia is typically done at least once a year; electronic updates are normally provided more frequently.

Format is a significant element in evaluating encyclopedias for library media centers. With the evolution of electronic encyclopedias, the criteria have altered somewhat; however, many of the same points should be considered as for print encyclopedias. Are the illustrations (charts and maps) current, functional, clear, easy to follow, and appropriate for the intended audience? Are the motion and sound (electronic formats) functional, clear, and suitable for the intended users? Do the motion and sound enhance the text or are they merely "fun"? Is it easy to locate information quickly and easily? The format of an encyclopedia should not interfere with the purpose. In making their choices, library media specialists need to decide if the product is appropriate for the needs and characteristics of the school, student population, and community served.

A detailed *index* is an absolute necessity. Indexing is any means by which the user can be directed to the fullest range of information. Some children's encyclopedias include at the end of each volume an index that refers to pages within the volume as well as to related information in other volumes.

We are apt to assume that all encyclopedias are *objective*. This is not the case. One should check for objectivity and biases. Are both sides of a controversial issue represented? Be alert to passive or implicit biases as well, such as stereotyping. Notice what is excluded, what is emphasized, and what is de-emphasized. Compare the size of one article with another. Remember that encyclopedias are published as a profit venture.

Usually the *scope* of encyclopedias makes them ideal for reference work. The purpose is defined in terms of audience (age level) and emphasis (content and the way the content is presented). Who is the encyclopedia really for? Is it truly appropriate for the age group it claims to serve? It is extremely difficult for an encyclopedia to be equally useful for children and adults. Currently, emphasis is essentially a matter of deciding what compromise will be made between scholarship and popularity. Subject coverage should be uniform from discipline to discipline. Check the proportional length and depth of subjects as well as the inclusion of contemporary issues.

The *selection* of encyclopedias appropriate for a library media center will depend entirely on the needs and requirements of the students served. Typically, encyclopedias provide information that is relatively general, clearly written, and free of jargon and complicated technical terminology. Generally speaking, library media centers have a great need for all types of encyclopedias. Use selection tools to determine the most suitable encyclopedias for your situation. *Kister's Concise Guide to Best Encyclopedias* (Oryx Press) is an excellent selection aid, containing comparison charts of encyclopedias' currency, authority, reliability, purpose, objectivity and history. "Reference Books Bulletin" in *Booklist* (American Library Association) provides detailed and timely reviews about encyclopedias on a periodic basis.

Cost is another crucial factor in selecting encyclopedias. Although costs vary, print or CD-ROM formats of encyclopedias are similar in that one buys ownership, unlimited use, and then purchases updates on a cyclical basis. Often CD-ROM encyclopedias provide updates at a reduced rate. When purchasing online encyclopedias, remember you pay for only the information retrieved.

There are significant variations in cost when considering print, CD-ROM or online formats of encyclopedias. Online sources have the potential of being updated more frequently. Above all else, always consider the needs and abilities of the students you serve when selecting encyclopedias.

Basic Sources

Traditional General Encyclopedias. For children and young adults, the most notable print encyclopedia is *World Book*, known for its reliability, logical organization, and ease of use. It includes a good balance between text and 29,000 timely illustrations. Each article concludes with a study aid. Target ages are 10-16.

The most significant CD-ROM encyclopedias for school library media centers include *Compton's Interactive Encyclopedia* (Compton's), *The New Grolier Multimedia Encyclopedia* and *Encarta* (Microsoft Corporation). *Compton's* contains over 100 video clips and animations (some in 3-D) as well as the 65,000-word *Merriam-Webster Intermediate Dictionary*. *Grolier's* CD-ROM contains over six hours of sound, 100 video clips, animation, and maps. *Encarta* provides eight hours of sound, over 100 video clips, animation, and a dictionary and thesaurus. All of these encyclopedias are excellent choices for library media centers.

Other appropriate examples of encyclopedias for children and young adults include:

- *World Book Multimedia Encyclopedia* (World Book, CD-ROM format),
- *Collier's Encyclopedia* (Collier's, print format),
- *Academic American Encyclopedia* (Grolier's, print format),
- *Funk & Wagnall's New Encyclopedia* (Funk & Wagnall's, print format),
- *Grolier's The New Book of Knowledge* (Grolier's, print format),
- *Oxford Children's Encyclopedia* (Oxford University Press, print format),
- *Children's Britannica* (Britannica, print format),
- *Childcraft* (World Book, print format), and
- *First Connections: The Golden Book Encyclopedia* (Hartley Courseware, CD-ROM format).

Britannica Encyclopedia is now available online (**www.britannica.com**). This user-friendly encyclopedia allows users to search and read the full text of the *Encyclopedia Britannica*. *Microsoft Encarta Concise Encyclopedia* is another example of an online source (**http://encarta.msn.com/default.asp**). This free, concise encyclopedia contains 16,000 articles and 72,200 photographs, illustrations, maps, charts, and tables. *Grolier Multimedia Encyclopedia Online* (**http://gme.grolier.com/**) is yet another online example. This encyclopedia is fee-based; free trials are available.

Single-Volume Encyclopedias are enjoying a resurgence in popularity. They meet the needs of students interested in a single fact, place, or phenomenon. They are concise works of information excellent for ready-reference, factual questions. The following are examples of single-volume encyclopedias suitable for school library media centers:

- *Webster's New World Encyclopedia* (Prentice-Hall, print format),
- *Random House Encyclopedia* (Random House, print and CD-ROM formats),
- *The Random House Children's Encyclopedia* (Random House, print format),
- *The Cambridge Encyclopedia* (Cambridge University Press, print format), and
- *The Barnes and Noble Encyclopedia* (Barnes and Noble, print format).

Subject Encyclopedias. For every general encyclopedia available, there are dozens of subject works. Reviews of subject encyclopedias can be read in *Library Journal* (Reed Elsevier Inc.), *Choice* (American Library Association), and *Booklist* (American Library Association) journals. Information pertaining to these reference sources is also available in *Kister's Best Encyclopedias* (Oryx Press).

There are innumerable subject encyclopedias in existence, over 1,000 in the English language alone. The following well-known and popular sources, typically found in library media centers, are examples of subject encyclopedias covering a variety of topics and areas of interest:

- *McGraw-Hill Concise Encyclopedia of Science and Technology* (McGraw-Hill, print format);
- *Eyewitness Encyclopedia of Science* (Dorling Kindersley, CD-ROM format);

- *Mammals: A Multimedia Encyclopedia* (National Geographic Society, CD-ROM format);

- *Encyclopedia of Psychology* (Wiley Interscience, print format);

- *Eyewitness History of the World* (Ivan R. Dee Publishing, CD-ROM format);

- *Encyclopedia of American History* (HarperCollins, print format);

- *McGraw-Hill Encyclopedia of World Drama* (McGraw-Hill, print format);

- *Encyclopedia of the Renaissance* (Charles Scribner's Sons, print format);

- *The Encyclopedia of World Art* (McGraw-Hill, print format);

- *Microsoft Art Gallery* (Microsoft Corporation, CD-ROM format);

- *Benet's Readers' Encyclopedia* (HarperCollins, print format);

- *The Middle Ages: An Encyclopedia for Students* (Charles Scribner's Sons, print format);

- *McGraw-Hill Encyclopedia of World Biography* (McGraw-Hill, print format); and

- *Encyclopedia of Poetry and Poetics* (Princeton University Press, print format).

Encyclopedias of all types are essential reference sources for school library media centers. General traditional, single-volume, and subject encyclopedias provide answers—a systematic overview of selected topics—a picture of how things were and are.

Chapter 7

Geographical Sources

Introduction

Geographical reference sources can be thought of as works of art. They provide aesthetic satisfaction and the opportunity to let one's imagination wander. These reference materials are used primarily to answer location questions. Geographical sources may be used at an uncomplicated level (for example, Where is the country of Qatar?) or at a more sophisticated level involving relationships among environment, history, climate, and political boundaries (for example, How has the melting of the polar ice caps affected climate in the Northern Hemisphere?)

Human society has become more global than ever before; therefore, current geographical resources are a necessity. When a student wants to identify a geographic place, normally the answer can be found in an atlas or an individual map. Some questions may require extremely up-to-date geographical materials; atlases, maps, and other resources should be specifically selected for questions about current events. Responding to the need for current information may require the use of online resources.

Other geographical questions involve history. Information of this nature can be located in older atlases and related geographical sources. Therefore, age need not be a reason for weeding geographical materials. Geographical requests can vary widely, requiring an assortment of geography-related sources such as current, historical, and thematic atlases; maps of varying types such as gazetteers and travel guides; and even general reference materials, like encyclopedias, that include geographic information.

With the wealth of geographical sources currently online and on CD-ROMs, it is now easier to answer students' diverse geographical questions. The categories of geographical sources considered in this chapter include print and electronic maps, atlases, gazetteers, and other general geographical sources appropriate for school library media centers.

Maps are representations of certain boundaries on a flat surface. However, there are maps designed for every purpose, from indicating soil content to determining the vegetation in a particular city via satellite imaging. A physical map traces the features of the land—rivers and valleys, mountains and hills. A street (route) map shows roads, railroads, bridges, and similar structures. A map depicting specific conditions is typically referred to as a thematic map. These, either separately or as one, make up a large number of maps found in atlases.

An *atlas* is simply a volume of maps. Atlases can provide the whole world in one book at a nominal cost. Individual atlases cover numerous subjects and offer reference information on geographical features, oceans, space, and historical and political geography of particular areas. Atlases may be divided into three categories: current, historical, and thematic.

Gazetteers or geographic dictionaries provide information regarding place-names. Often they include information on population, climate, and economy. Electronic geographic sources (CD-ROMs and online formats) are becoming a regular and vitally important part of school library media reference resources. These sources serve a multitude of valuable functions, are typically user-friendly, and are remarkably current. Often electronic and print geographic materials complement each other. This chapter will discuss all formats of geographic resources.

Evaluation and Selection

Geographic sources may be evaluated using many of the same criteria as other reference sources; however, there are several additional points to consider. Because these materials depend on graphic arts and mathematics, evaluation and selection must involve further issues. The basic criteria to be considered when evaluating geographic resources are publisher (authority), scale, currency, indexing, and format.

With geographic resources, as with any reference area, there exist competent and reputable publishers. In the United States, the leading publishers include Rand McNally, C. S. Hammond, and the National Geographic Society. Prominent international publishers include John Bartholomew and Oxford University Press. When the publisher's reputation is unknown, it is wise to inspect other works by that publisher. This is particularly important with electronic geographic sources, where the vendor or publisher may not be one of the standard companies. Numerous smaller firms produce geographic materials, in particular, city maps. In all cases it is best to purchase resources from reliable publishers or locally reputable organizations. Also, remember that geography is a component of numerous other reference materials such as encyclopedias and almanacs. It is important that the publisher of the encyclopedia have a reliable reputation as well.

Scale is a characteristic that makes geographic resources different from other reference materials. Maps are usually classified according to scale. Scale is the most important element of a map, as it defines the amount of information that can be shown, as well as the size of the geographic area. One unit on a map equals a particular number of units on the ground (for example, one inch equals 10 miles). The scale from map to map in a given atlas may vary widely, although better atlases attempt to standardize their work. An effective map or atlas identifies the scale; as a school library media specialist, you decide the appropriate scale for your student population.

Evaluation of Geographic Sources

AUTHORITY

- Purchase from a reputable publisher of geographic materials.
- If the publisher is unknown, examine other works published by the same firm.

SCALE

- Scale is the most important element, as it defines the amount of information that can be shown.
- The scale should be clearly defined and appropriate for the intended audience.

CURRENCY

- Geographic names and boundaries change rapidly: A five-year-old atlas is considered "historical."

INDEXING

- A comprehensive index is important.
- An effective geographical index is an alphabetical list of all place-names that appear on the map.
- Electronic geographical sources should provide rapid and user-friendly access to information.

FORMAT

- Regardless of format, geographic resources must provide the desired information quickly and easily, which requires that they be clear and legible.

Another essential criterion for geographic resources is *currency*. Because the world is changing so rapidly, it is of utmost importance that the school library media center provide up-to-date geographical information. School library media specialists should update their world maps frequently, although electronic formats are now supplying current information on a regular basis. A world atlas that is five years old portrays enough obsolete information to be considered only for historical purposes. A multitude of changes occur on a continual basis regarding geographical sources—place-names, boundaries, roads. Revisions of maps and atlases (complete overhaul and redevelopment) normally take place every 10 years—the equivalent of the American decennial census.

An effective geographical *index* is an alphabetical list of all place-names that appear on the map. A comprehensive index is as important in geographic reference work as the maps themselves. It should consist of a reference to the exact map as well as latitude, longitude, and grid information. Indexes may also include such features as national parks, mountains, and historical sites. An effective atlas or map indexes as many features as possible. Online and CD-ROM software should provide rapid and user-friendly access to the information it includes.

Geographic sources in any *format* should provide the desired information as quickly and easily as possible; it must be clear and legible. Maps with fewer items of information are typically easier to read; the actual number of points represented on a map is a major editorial decision.

Electronic geographic sources are increasingly important and necessary. There are numerous high-quality and user-friendly electronic materials. National Geographic's online site (**www.nationalgeographic.com/maps/index.html**) is an excellent source, offering "Dynamic Maps," "Atlas Maps," "Flags and Facts," satellite imaging, and many other useful features. Rand McNally's online site (**www.randmcnally.com**) is also a valuable source for planning trips, exploring maps, and finding addresses and driving directions. The format of geographical sources should be selected on the basis of student needs and abilities, as well as relative cost.

In choosing geographical reference materials, each school library media specialist must determine the informational requirements and desires of the school, student population, and community served. However, locating suitable selection tools and aids in this field is more difficult than in other reference areas. Several journals review geographical sources (some on a regular basis; some sporadically) such as *Booklist* (American Library Association), *The Book Report* (Linworth Publishing, Inc.), *Library Journal* (Reed Elsevier Inc.), *Library Talk* (Linworth Publishing, Inc.) and *School Library Journal* (Reed Elsevier Inc.). An additional valuable tool is *A Geographical Bibliography for American Libraries* (Association of American Geographers). This aid contains a section, "For School Libraries," that recommends titles for elementary and secondary schools. Each entry is annotated, and a useful index provides access to authors, short titles, and subjects.

Basic Sources

Current World Atlases are required for up-to-date information on geographical and political changes in the world. Many students find print versions of atlases enjoyable as well as useful. Probably the most notable single-volume world atlas (print format) is the *Times Atlas of the World* (Random House), which consists of 18 maps of North America, 40 of Europe, 34 of Asia, 12 of Africa, and seven of Latin America. The *Times Atlas of the World* is divided into three basic sections: an introduction with general physical information, the atlas proper with a series of regional maps, and a final index-gazetteer section. The *New York Times Atlas* (Random House, print format) is a smaller version of the *Times Atlas of the World* that offers balanced coverage, and because it is moderately priced is a good choice for school library media centers.

The medium-sized atlas, *Hammond's Atlas of the World* (Hammond Inc., print format), is also appropriate for school populations. This atlas contains 160 pages of maps including thematic maps illustrating global relationships, as well as several text sections on such topics as the environment and the development of cartography. It gives relative balance to the nations of the globe. Another medium-sized current atlas suitable for school library media centers is the *National Geographic Atlas* (National Geographic Society, print format) containing excellent thematic maps, graphics, and vivid comparisons between geographic locations. *Goode's World Atlas* (Rand McNally), a desk-sized atlas in print format, reasonably priced and easy to use, is often found in library media centers. *Goode'* is revised every other year; its serviceable index has 36,000 entries.

Rand McNally's America: Family United States Atlas (Rand McNally, CD-ROM format) is a true multimedia atlas offering sound, pictures, and text, as well as a complete summary of American demographic information. The *Picture Atlas of the World* (National Geographic Society, CD-ROM format) is published by the National Geographic Society. This CD-ROM atlas includes over 800 maps, 1,200 photographs, and 50 video clips. Maps of each country are complemented with text about vital statistics and history. The *Small Blue Planet* (Now What Software, CD-ROM format) atlas consists of three primary parts: standard maps, satellite images, and a world political map with historical and statistical data. This atlas is user-friendly and developed with the young adult in mind. Offering most of the same features is *Encarta Interactive World Atlas* by Microsoft Corporation, part of the CD-ROM Microsoft Reference Suite 2000.

Numerous online atlases also exist, many of them as a part of other reference sources such as *Grolier's Encyclopedia* (**http://publishing.grolier.com/**). *Compton's 3D Atlas Online* (**www.3datlas.com/main_about.html**) is an excellent example of an electronic atlas. *Compton's* provides timely world news, best research links for every country, and a geographic glossary. Two additional examples of online atlases are the *Map Machine Atlas* (**http://plasma.nationalgeographic.com/mapmachine/**) and *The Lonely Planet* (**www.lonelyplanet.com**).

Historical Atlases are necessary for the study of early exploration, boundary changes, and military campaigns. The *Historical Atlas of the 20th Century,* an online source (**http://users.erols.com/mwhite28/20centry.htm**), charts socioeconomic trends, systems of government, cities, and wars throughout the 20th century. The *Historical Atlas of the United States* (National Geographic Society, print format) includes hundreds of maps, over 450 photographs, 180 graphs, and 140,000 words of text. Numerous other historical atlases are useful for library media centers. They vary in content, concentrating on either particular periods in history or specific regions.

Examples of historical atlases suitable for school library media centers include:

- *Atlas of Russian History* (Oxford University Press),
- *Hammond's American History Atlas* (Hammond Incorporated),
- *Atlas of Classical History* (Routledge),
- *Historical Atlas of the American West* (University of Oklahoma Press),
- *National Geographic Society Historical Atlas of the United States* (National Geographic Society),
- *The Oxford Illustrated History of the British Monarchy* (Oxford University Press),
- *Atlas of British History* (Oxford University Press), and
- *The Atlas of American History* (Checkmark Books).

Thematic Atlases, emphasizing a specific subject or region, represent a new trend in atlas publishing. Although they are considered atlases, many thematic atlases more closely resemble finely illustrated popular histories. The *Atlas of North America* (IDG Books Worldwide) has an unusual blend of traditional maps and satellite imagery. It includes black and white, natural-color, and infrared images, as well as geographical information on North America.

Further examples of thematic atlases appropriate for school library media centers include:

- *The West Point Atlas of American Wars* (Henry Holt and Company),
- *The Pacific War Atlas* (Facts on File),
- *The Atlas of Endangered Resources* (Checkmark Books),
- *Atlas of the North American Indian* (Checkmark Books),
- *Atlas of the Arab World* (Facts on File),
- *Atlas of the Bible* (Facts on File),
- *Atlas of the Holocaust* (William Morrow),
- *Atlas of the Roman World* (Checkmark Books),
- *Cultural Atlas of Japan* (Checkmark Books),
- *Rand McNally's Children's Atlas of World Wildlife* (Rand McNally), and
- *Cultural Atlas of France* (Checkmark Books).

Maps. At least 90 percent of the maps published each year originate from government sources. The United States Geological Survey (USGS) is the agency officially responsible for domestic mapping. Of all the USGS series, the topographical maps are the best known and most used. They show in great detail the physical features of an area. School library media centers may request free state indexes and other state-specific information by calling 1-800-USA-MAPS.

Most municipal governments and regional agencies produce maps for planning and engineering studies. Government information can be found online at numerous sites; two examples are (**www.libraryspot.com/governmentlibraries.htm**) and (**www.library.vanderbilt.edu/central/govt/gvtindx.html**). These maps are typically free or available at a reasonable reproduction cost. Chambers of Commerce usually have detailed city maps as well as other information on their cities; they are excellent resources for library media centers. State departments of

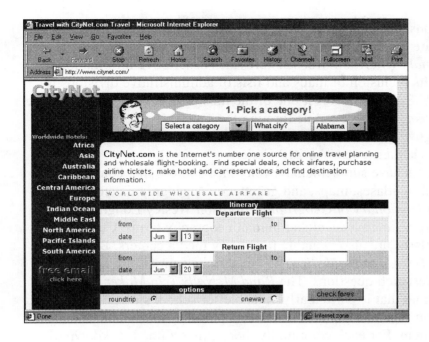

tourism are also good sources of maps; most can be found online (for instance, the online source for Kentucky is **www.kytourism.com**).

Many online sites exist for maps of all kinds. It is important to remember, however, that it is sometimes difficult to "get the big picture" on a computer screen. In addition, printing can be a challenge. Nonetheless, these resources—valuable for school library media centers—are typically free of charge. One large, useful online source is *CityNet* (**www.citynet.com**), which provides access to information on travel, entertainment, local businesses, and government and community services for all regions of the world.

Other examples of online map sources are:

■ *Maps in the News* (**www-map.lib.umn.edu/news.html**),

■ *MapBlast* (**www.mapblast.com/mblast/index.mb**),

■ *Maps on Us* (**www.mapsonus.com/**), and

■ *Yahoo Maps* (**www.maps.yahoo.com/py/maps.py**).

When you evaluate a local map, consider the following:

■ Is it truly local?

■ Does it show the area in detail?

■ Is it large-scale?

■ Is it current?

■ Is it appropriate for student use?

Gazetteers and Other Geographical Sources. A gazetteer is a list of geographical names and physical features. It is a geographical dictionary for finding lists of cities, mountains, rivers, populations, and other features. Almost every atlas includes a gazetteer as an appendix that is used to locate the place-names in that volume. Atlas gazetteers are primarily useful for locating major towns, cities, administrative divisions, and physical features. Gazetteers differ from the index to an atlas in that they are generally more comprehensive. *Webster's New Geographical Dictionary* (Merriam-Webster) provides descriptive information for numerous locations. Its inclusion of maps and lists of administrative divisions for major countries and U.S. states makes it one of the most useful gazetteers available today. The *US Gazetteer,* available online through the Tiger Map Server (**http://tiger.census.gov/**) is an excellent example of an electronic gazetteer, identifying locations via name, state, or ZIP Code.

Geographical items have supplementary reference sources that contain information not found in atlases, maps, and gazetteers. A geographic encyclopedia such as the *Longman Dictionary of Geography* (Addison Wesley Longman) is a useful resource, incorporating physical and human geography terms. Current street and road maps and atlases are also valuable for library media centers. Both print (such as *Road Atlas: US, Canada, Mexico*) and electronic formats are helpful for ready-reference and research questions. The *Rand McNally Trip Maker* is a street map in CD-ROM format that is particularly valuable for school situations. Using this map, a student can type in a point of origin and point of destination; the route is then drawn on the map. For each community there exists a fine breakdown of streets and major sites. This resource is moderately priced and updated for a nominal cost each year.

Road Maps (**www.avis.com/maps_and_directions/road_maps/**) is an example of an online street map. *MapQuest* (**www.mapquest.com/**), another online resource, enables one to find a specific location and obtain driving directions or plan a trip to that destination. Further examples of electronic street or road maps include *Lycos Road Map* (**www.lycos.com/roadmap.html**) and *Microsoft Expedia Maps* (**http://maps.expedia.com/OverView.asp**).

Travel guidebooks are valuable geographic resources for school library media centers. They deal with down-to-earth facts about specific locations. The most notable publishers of travel guidebooks include *Frommer, Fodor, Fielding,* and *Dorling Kindersley.*

As stimulating as geographic materials are for the imaginative mind, they are also an invaluable part of any school library media center reference collection. As a library media specialist, you will find there are as many reasons for consulting geographic resources as there are students in your school. With the introduction of electronic maps and atlases, reference work involving geographic materials has become an exciting and challenging aspect of the school library media specialist's services.

Chapter *8*

Indexes and Abstracts

Introduction

Whether separate guides to periodical articles or part of books, indexes guide the user to specific information in a larger unit. An index is an analysis of a document, typically by subject. An effective index includes enough access points to allow the user to locate precisely what is needed. A large majority of indexes today are electronic.

Abstracts are an extension of indexes. They present a brief, objective summary of content and help the user assess the content of a document. Abstracts provide enough information to give the user an accurate idea about the subject area. They are usually descriptive, as opposed to evaluative. A typical abstract is from 100 to 300 words long. An effective abstract, by itself, may include more than enough information to answer a ready-reference question.

More and more publications are now in full text either on CD-ROM or online; the text is searchable for incidences of the keywords sought. Electronic formats have numerous advantages, such as rapid search of a number of indexes; the ability to move from citation to abstract to full text; and more points of access through keywords in the title, text, or specific periodical.

Evaluation and Selection

Indexes and abstracts should be evaluated and selected so as to best reveal the contents of the collection and most efficiently refer students to requested information not found in the school library media center. Evaluation of print or electronic indexes and abstracts follows many of the same rules as other reference sources. The basic difference lies in the ease in retrieving data. In evaluating indexes and abstracts, consider accuracy, authority, format, and scope.

A misleading index or inaccurate abstract can cause a multitude of problems.

Accuracy must be the paramount consideration. Make sure all major facets of an article's content are represented by entries in the subject index, and all authors connected with the indexed item are included in the author index. Author names should be spelled the same way in the index and the work itself. Subjects should represent the content of the publication; cross-references should be included as needed. Effective abstracts must accurately summarize the original article's content.

The *authority* of indexes and abstracts relates to the reputation of the publisher or sponsoring agency. Three prominent publishers of indexes are

Evaluation of Indexes and Abstracts

AUTHORITY

- Authority primarily relies on the reputation of the publisher or sponsoring agency.
- Three prominent publishers are EBSCO, H.W. Wilson, and University Microfilm International (UMI).
- For electronic resources, verify authority by talking to subject experts and reading relevant reviews.
- Make sure the publisher or vender supplies the necessary documentation, frequent updates, and information regarding current changes.

ACCURACY

- An inaccurate index can cause a multitude of problems.
- All major facets of the content in the article should be represented by entries in the subject index.
- All authors affiliated with the indexed item should be included in the author index.
- Author names should be spelled identically in the index and the work itself.
- Subjects should represent the content of the publication.
- Effective abstracts should accurately summarize the original article's content.

FORMAT

- When you evaluate electronic sources, consider both ease of searching and consistency of procedures with the vendor's or publisher's other indexes.
- Insist on readability in both print and electronic formats.
- Consider type size and style (font) and clarity of abbreviations and symbols.

SCOPE

- An index should adequately cover the materials in the field of interest.
- Consider the frequency of the publication and its cumulative versions, the number of subjects covered, and the types of materials indexed.
- Be aware of possible duplications and overlaps.

EBSCO, H. W. Wilson, and University Microfilm International (UMI). As more electronic indexes appear, additional publishers will emerge; verify their reputations by talking to subject experts and reading reviews. With electronic resources it is equally important to ascertain the reputation of the vendor and producer (not necessarily the same as the publisher). Expect the publisher or vendor to supply necessary documentation, frequent updates, and information about current changes.

As for *format*, most indexes and abstracts now exist in electronic form. When evaluating these resources, consider ease of searching and determine whether procedures are consistent throughout all of the vendor's or publisher's indexes (either on CD-ROM or online). Because some databases do not cover material before the mid-1960s, you may need print versions for searching older literature. Readability is essential for both print and electronic formats. Type should be large enough, abbreviations and symbols should be understandable, and boldface type should be used effectively. Also consider arrangement with print indexes and abstracts; with electronic sources, the search engine will normally reveal the location of a term regardless of where it is.

Determine the *scope* of indexes and abstracts you are considering for purchase. Does it adequately cover the materials in the subject indexed or abstracted? Take into account frequency of publication and of cumulative editions. (Typically electronic indexes and abstracts are periodically accumulated automatically.) Other considerations are number of subjects covered and types of materials indexed. Indexes and abstracts vary in the number of publications they include and the depth of the coverage they provide. Some are inclusive as to the types of materials indexed; others restrict their coverage to particular titles. As there are many indexes available today, be aware of possible duplications and overlaps in information.

The *selection* of indexes and abstracts for a school library media center depends on the needs of the students and the characteristics of the current collection. Many standard resources will serve as aids in the selection of indexes and abstracts. Examples are:

■ *Guide to Reference Materials for School Media Centers* (Libraries Unlimited),

■ *Reference Books for Children* (Scarecrow Press), and

■ *The Elementary School Library Collection: A Guide to Books and Other Media* (Brodart).

Additionally, review journals such as the following will include information on indexes and abstracts:

■ *Booklist* (American Library Association),

■ *The Book Report* (Linworth Publishing),

■ *Choice* (American Library Association),

■ *Library Journal* (Reed Elsevier Inc.),

■ *Library Talk* (Linworth Publishing), and

■ *School Library Journal* (Reed Elsevier Inc.)

Cost and student needs are the most critical factors in selecting indexes and abstracts. These resources are usually expensive. However, most school library media centers do not require very many. Consider whether the index will provide full-text articles. An index is of little use if the library does not have access to the periodicals indexed. Abstracts are typically helpful only for brief facts and ready-reference questions. The variation in price of electronic databases can be difficult to understand; licensing is one of the variables. Vendors' and publishers' fees for library media centers depend on the number of users and how they are using the system.

The indexes and abstracts purchased should reflect the types of information students need. School library media centers need general periodical and newspaper indexes, but online indexes and abstracts make numerous indexes available without subscription. Many school library media centers now have online indexes and abstracts available through library consortia, such as statewide library networks.

Basic Sources

Current, well-known indexes and abstracts appropriate for school library media centers may be divided into two categories: magazines and newspapers, and specialized indexes. As there are countless indexes and abstracts available today, the following are merely examples. The first four series, *ProQuest, EBSCO, SIRS,* and *NewsBank* are fee-based services.

Magazines and Newspapers. One popular publisher of indexes is Bell & Howell, whose best-known indexes are the *ProQuest* series. These indexes are offered online (**www.proquest.com**), on CD-ROM, and in microform. The online collection is a Web-based service that lets users locate magazines, newspapers, and topical reference information quickly and easily. It is delivered in abstract and full-text. The following are examples of the *ProQuest* collection:

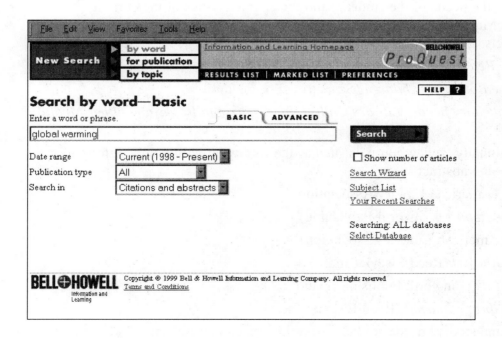

- *ProQuest KidQuest* provides access to over 100 periodicals, many of them full-text and includes charts, photos, drawings, and other graphics. This kid-friendly index emphasizes nature, science, and educational topics. Students can select from broad topic areas, such as health, sports, people, plants and animals, and cultural issues. *ProQuest KidQuest* also includes the "Reference Module," which features the *World Book Encyclopedia, CIA Fact Book, Occupational Outlook Handbook,* and *Ethnic Cultures of America.*

- *ProQuest JuniorQuest* includes access to over 120 core periodicals (90 percent full-text) targeted at middle-school research. It provides full-text newspaper coverage, charts, graphs, photos, and other graphics, as well as the previously mentioned "Reference Module."

- *ProQuest Bronze, Silver, Gold,* and *Platinum* all offer coverage on popular journal titles (*Bronze* having the least; *Platinum* having the most—over 2000 periodicals), full-text coverage of numerous newspapers, daily updates, and cumulative material that provides up-to-the-minute reports. The "Reference Module" is also included.

- The *ProQuest* interface allows students to search single or multiple databases, provides integrated subject lists, includes flexible search options, and offers a user-friendly version designed specifically for K-12 students.

  EBSCO is another leading publisher of indexes and abstracts (**www-us.ebsco.com/home/school.htm**).

- *EBSCO Primary/Elementary Searchasaurus* (online and CD-ROM formats), for elementary-age students, indexes more than 50 magazines of interest to this age level. Through this index, the student may choose *Primary/Elementary, Middle Search Plus, Encyclopedia of Animals,* and a *General Encyclopedia.* The

Searchasaurus can be searched by word or subject (literature, sports, nature).

- *EBSCO Middle Search Plus Searchasaurus* (online and CD-ROM formats) indexes 200 magazines of interest to middle school students; 100 of them are full-text. It is updated weekly; access to data is obtained in the same manner as *Primary Searchasaurus.*

- *EBSCO High School Search* (online and CD-ROM formats) includes over 500 publications suitable for high school students. Full-text is available for over 200 of the journals. *EBSCO Topic Search* (online and CD-ROM formats), for middle and high school students, includes 40,000 full-text documents from 72,500 sources.

- *EBSCOhost Masterfile Elite* (online) indexes and abstracts over 2,700 magazines and newspapers; 1,200 are full-text.

Two other indexes include *MAS FullTEXT Ultra,* which provides full-text for approximately 600 magazines, and *MasterFILE Premier*, which includes full text of 1,960 periodicals in many subject areas.

The *Social Issues Resource Series (SIRS Mandarin, Inc.),* (**www.sirs.com/**) is an online resource giving integrated access to thousands of full-text articles from magazines, scholarly journals, newspapers, and government documents. The databases can be searched either simultaneously or individually. *SIRS* also provides "Research Strategy Worksheets," which review searching strategies and Boolean operators. *SIRS* offers four different indexes: *SIRS Discoverer, SIRS Researcher, SIRS Government Reporter* and *SIRS Renaissance.*

- *SIRS Discoverer* comes in three editions: elementary, middle, and deluxe. It is an interactive database. Because it includes elementary and middle school curriculum topics, it can easily be integrated into classroom activities. This index, developed with the young researcher in mind, strengthens research skills. *Discoverer* also includes elementary and middle school education workbooks and a comprehensive educator's guide.

- *SIRS Researcher* is a general reference database of thousands of full-text articles covering social, scientific, health, historic, economic, business, political, and global issues. The articles are selected from more than 1,500 domestic and international newspapers, magazines, journals, and government publications; they are archived from 1989 to present.

- *SIRS Government Reporter* contains thousands of full-text articles pertaining to health, science, economics, environment, politics, foreign affairs, business and industry, both current and historical. The almanac databases are valuable tools for researching current and historic government documents, United States Supreme Court decisions, elected leaders, and the like.

- *SIRS Renaissance* includes current, dynamic information on music, literature, film, performing arts, culture, architecture, religion, and visual arts. Many of the articles are accompanied by full-color graphics. It is an excellent resource for both in-depth reports and browsing.

NewsBank is another popular indexing series (**www.newsbank.com/schools/**). *NewsBank SchoolMate,* appropriate for elementary and middle school students, includes over 500 newspapers and 30 magazines. *SchoolMate KidsPage* for elementary students (grades two and up) is updated daily and has colorful icons and simple vocabulary. The articles indexed are from newspapers and magazines of interest to young readers; the index includes lesson plans and student projects. *SchoolMate* for middle school students is a cross-curricular database covering numerous subject areas. It includes articles from over 500 local, regional, and national newspapers and 30 magazines with a broad range of reading levels. *SchoolMate* is retrospective from 1992 to present and offers flexible search options. *Curriculum Resource by NewsBank* is an integrated, cross-curricular database that supports many areas of study. The information is selected specifically for its instructional value and curricular relevance. This index is appropriate for high school students and adults.

Numerous additional online sources provide guides to newspapers and magazines. One of these is *AJR News Link (American Journalism Review)* at (**http://ajr.newslink.org/**), which contains comprehensive links to international newspapers and magazines on the Internet. Newspapers published in the United States are arranged by state. *AJR* also contains links to radio and television resources in the United States and other countries. Another online source is located at the *Internet Public Library* (**www.ipl.org/reading/serials**). Such resources as *Online Newspapers, Online Serials, News and Newspapers Online, My Virtual Reference Desk—My Virtual Newspaper,* the *Los Angeles Times,* and the *New York Times* can be accessed through this Web site. *Newspapers Online* (**www.newspapers.com/**) is yet another valuable source that includes free access to the world's top 100 newspapers.

The *Children's Magazine Guide* (print format), an excellent resource for children ages 8 to 12, indexes 51 popular children's magazines with articles on sports, science, popular culture, and current events. *Children's Magazine Guide* provides nine monthly issues and an annual cumulative edition.

Specialized Indexes. Besides general indexes and abstracts, there are specialized indexes on a wide range of subjects. The following are examples of specialized indexes appropriate for school library media centers:

The Educational Resources Information Center (ERIC) is a federally funded national information system that provides a variety of services and products on a broad range of education-related issues. The world's largest source of educational information, *ERIC* contains more than one million abstracts of documents and journal articles on educational research and practice. This online database (**www.accesseric.org**) is updated monthly; the information is timely and accurate. *ERIC* may be consulted for both original and secondary material on education. The system includes:

■ Indexes to unpublished reports (*Resources in Education*) and to journals (*Current Index to Journals in Education* or *CIJE*, which indexes approximately 775 periodicals in education);

■ A subject vocabulary represented in the frequently updated *Thesaurus of ERIC Descriptors*; and

■ A decentralized organizational structure for acquiring and processing the documents that are indexed and abstracted.

Resources in Education lists nearly 15,000 unpublished reports and associated items per year. Each entry has a narrative abstract of approximately 200 words. The reports are divided nearly equally among three categories: research and technical reports; proceedings, dissertations, preprints, and papers printed at conferences; and curriculum guides, educational legislation, and lesson plans.

ERIC is an excellent place to begin to learn about a subject. Some subjects are not found elsewhere. The reports are usually complete with bibliographies, readings, and suggestions for further research.

AskERIC is a personalized Internet-based service providing educational information to teachers, librarians, counselors, administrators, parents, and others throughout the world. *AskERIC* began in 1992 and today encompasses the resources of the entire *ERIC* system and more. The main components of *AskERIC* are *AskERIC Question and Answer Service, AskERIC Virtual Library* (which includes selected educational resources and over 1,000 *AskERIC* lesson plans), and *AskERIC InfoGuides* (searchable archives of education-related listservs, links to television series, and much more).

H. W. Wilson Company offers more than 40 full-text abstract and index databases in print, over the Internet (**www.hwwilson.com**), and on CD-ROM. The education indexes include full-text articles from approximately 500 periodicals, monographs, and yearbooks since January 1996. Other H. W. Wilson indexes cover social sciences, art, essays and general literature, humanities, library literature and information science, and *Book Review Digest*.

Another index of value to school library media centers is the *Index to the United States Government Printing Office (GPO)* publications (1976 to present) (**www.gpo.gov**/). In addition to records of GPO materials received by libraries, *GPO* also includes the *Public Affairs Information Service (PAIS),* records of articles in 1,400 periodicals and thousands of government documents, statistical directories, reports, and books. *GPO* covers international materials from the entire spectrum of public and social policy issues: business, demographics, education, environment, health, and more.

The Columbia Granger's Index to Poetry (Columbia University Press, print and CD-ROM formats) is an index to more than 70,000 poems with a subject index of approximately 3,500 categories. An interesting feature of *Granger's* is the inclusion of 12,500 *last* lines, a valuable tool for searchers of quotations.

The *Short Story Index* (H. W. Wilson), available in print, CD-ROM and online formats (**www.hwwilson.com**), lists stories in both book collections and periodicals. This database indexes approximately 70,000 stories; 1,175 are offered online in full text. Information can be accessed via author, title, and subject for stories from collections; author and title for stories from periodicals. The information includes theme, locale, narrative technique, and genre.

The *Play Index* (H. W. Wilson, print format) is published every few years and includes more than 4,000 individual plays and plays in collections. Of importance to school library media centers, the *Play Index* uses tags, "c" for children through grade 6, and "y" for young adults in grades 7 to 12.

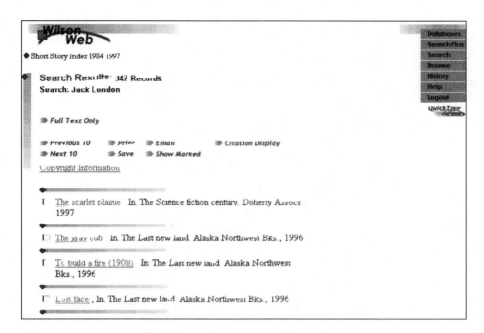

The average school library media center will typically not require more than one general index, because of the prohibitive cost and the fact that multiple indexes may well overlap and repeat. Prior to purchase, consult reviews, talk with vendors about their products, and gain some hands-on experience with the indexes themselves.

PART 3

The Art of
Questioning

Chapter **9**

The Reference Interview

Introduction

One of the primary functions of school library media specialists is to help students use the library and its collections. The first step, of course, is to determine what the students want. This process is referred to as the "reference interview"; it is an essential part of reference services and a major function of all school library media specialists. The reference interview is fundamentally a conversation between the library media specialist and the student for the purpose of clarifying the student's needs and meeting those needs (determining what they want). It is distinguished from general conversation between the library media specialist and student because it has a specific purpose and structure. In the reference interview, the library media specialist's goals are to determine efficiently and productively the nature, quantity, and level of information the student requires, as well as the most appropriate format.

The effective reference interview takes practice and creativity; it efficiently connects knowledge with the student's information needs. It is critical that library media specialists learn to listen and communicate with students effectively. As explained in *Information Power,* the school library media specialist "...is a catalyst in generating a spirit of inquiry within the learning community…. [B]y promoting careful and precise work at every stage of inquiry, the [library media specialist] underscores responsible information seeking and use" (69).

In discussing the reference interview, it is virtually impossible to divorce human relations from communications skills. It is vital to remember that librarians are dealing with humanism—bringing students and information together. It is up to each library media specialist to ensure that everything possible is done to keep the channels of communication open and flowing. As important as library media specialists are to students, students are even more important to librarians, for they are the lifeblood of our profession.

Each school library media specialist brings a distinctive personality and unique characteristics to the reference interview process. How these personalities and characteristics, both the school library media specialist's and the student's, affect the interview procedure are crucial. As library media specialists, we need to continually refine interviewing techniques and improve interpersonal skills. The reference interview bridges the communication gap between the student and the library media specialist.

In order to perform properly any reference service, the library media specialist must have an exceptional knowledge of the library media center's collection, both print and nonprint, to provide students with accurate, relevant information. In addition to knowledge of reference materials, the library media specialist should possess a complete knowledge of the general collection, as well as community resources.

Because questions differ, types of interviews vary also, as well as responses (from short and to the point to long and detailed). A successful reference interview is tailored to meet each student's needs. As school library media specialists, the types of interviews we perform most frequently are ready-reference, research projects, and readers' advisory. Each type of interview possesses its own unique qualities; however, all types serve the purpose of linking knowledge with student needs to promote learning.

Effective reference interviews have rules, methods, and characteristics that make the "connection" between information and student needs. Reference interviewing is not only an art, but also a science. It can be learned and practiced to produce effective results for students.

Your Patron—the Student

One of the most important aspects of the reference process (if not the most important) is attitude—how the student perceives his question will be received. It sets the mood for the entire transaction. It is important that the librarian comprehend the interview as a two-way communications system. School library media specialists work with a very special population—young people, students.

It has been observed that the deepest human need is to be appreciated. Keeping this in mind will make your work as a reference interviewer decidedly easier. As varied as students' reasons for and levels of questioning are, they have the same basic need—to protect or strengthen their self-concept. The school library media specialist should know as much about the student ("social data") as possible in order to conduct the most effective reference interview possible. This is not always easy, nor even possible. School library media specialists are in an exclusive position that allows them to gather data about their clientele prior to interviewing. However, not all information in an interview comes via the spoken word. Body language, tone of voice, and other verbal and nonverbal cues deliver meaning and help the interviewer discover what the student *wants*.

Each student comes to the reference interview with a distinctive question and an individual personality. But some "basic" considerations can be helpful in conducting a reference interview:

■ The student may not know what to expect, or the precise reaction the school library media specialist will have to the question.

■ The average student may have no foreknowledge of the type of resource(s) that will answer his or her question.

- The student's communications skills may not be as refined as the librarian's.
- The student may not know the terminology ("library lingo") used in the reference interview.
- The student may not specifically know what he or she is searching for because of a lack of knowledge about the subject or the assignment.
- The student may know little about the library media center's collection and policies.
- The student may misinterpret the library media specialist's nonverbal as well as verbal cues.
- The student may be fearful of the school library media specialist, or frustrated about the question being raised.

As a school library media specialist, remain aware that the reference interview is a two-way communication. Communication may become *mis*communication when a student is unable to verbalize his or her information need. As described by Kuhlthau, "The bibliographic paradigm is based on certainty and order, whereas [students'] problems are characterized by uncertainty and confusion" (361). It's the library media specialist's job to foster communication—discovering, understanding, and mastering the "art and science" of reference interviewing to connect knowledge with students' information needs.

The Setting

The physical setting in which the reference interview occurs affects its success. The environment of the school library media center conveys a message to the student. Library media specialists have some degree of control over the design and appearance of the library media center, both the reference collection (print and nonprint) and the physical setting. Comfort and utility are of foremost significance. Consider the following points in relation to the physical setting of the reference interview:

- Reference interviews should take place in a relatively quiet, uninterrupted area of the library media center that is comfortable and free of clutter.
- The reference area, the space in which the reference interview is conducted, should contain proper seating and be located near both print and nonprint reference sources.
- Reference materials should be organized in such a manner that the library media specialist and the student can easily locate reference sources during and after the reference interview.

The reference interview is a critical component of successful school librarianship. Reference services begin with an effective and productive interview. The physical setting is a distinct part of the interview and should be planned to enhance communication between the school library media specialist and the student.

You—the School Library Media Specialist

To conduct an appropriate and effective reference interview, you need specialized skills. Some of them can be taught, practiced, and learned. However, some skills are intangible—your individualism, your unique personality. Both tangible and intangible skills combine to create a successful reference interview.

Each school library media specialist wears a badge of individuality—his or her *style*. Style, an intangible feature, is a combination of attitudes, appearances, and experiences. As indefinable as style is, it plays a significant role in the reference interview. *Success* is another intangible feature of the reference interview that the library media specialist often overlooks. Sometimes successful interviews conclude without the student actually finding the necessary information—because the information does not exist, because the school library media center cannot provide the information, or even because the student did not require information in the first place. Regardless, a successful reference interview is one in which the student feels satisfied that the library media specialist has given personal attention and accurate information.

In addition to the intangible components, there are tangible skills—verbal and nonverbal—that library media specialists can identify and practice. Nonverbal communications assist the library media specialist to be approachable and interact positively with students. These skills, in many instances, are already a part of the *style* or demeanor of the library media specialist. Nonverbal skills—gestures, posture, facial expression, tone of voice, eye contact—are many times the easiest to learn and remember.

Verbal communications involve what is said as well as what is heard and understood by both the student and the library media specialist. Verbal skills are often more difficult to isolate and master. Once a verbal skill is learned, it should be reviewed and refined if one is to communicate more effectively. The skillful interviewer practices:

- Making positive (respectful) responses,
- Speaking motivational words (encouragers),
- Reflecting on what has been said,
- Reacting positively,
- Avoiding premature answers, diagnoses, or opinions,
- Restating or paraphrasing content,
- Remembering,
- Asking open questions, and
- Reaching closure.

Of primary importance throughout the interviewing procedure are careful listening and response. Talk to students as if they are important (because they are) and welcomed (which they should be). Take all questions seriously. Remember that appearance of attentiveness is essential for effective communication. In addition, it is crucial that the school library media specialist have a genuinely helpful attitude and commitment to growth and the pursuit of knowledge.

Being familiar with the library collection and finding sought-after information may be thought of as reference skills separate from the interview. They are, however, critical steps in the reference interview process. Without knowledge of the library media center collection, the interview cannot continue; the question cannot be answered. *Information Power's Information Access and Delivery* states that the school library media specialist should "...maintain current and in-depth knowledge about the complete range of educational and informational materials..." (85). Knowledge of the resources—general, reference, and community—creates the context in which the student can ask further questions as well as locate the desired information. The reference interview process relies on the reference interviewer's having a complex of skills to provide the most accurate and complete response—and ultimately, information.

Questions and Questioning

Speaking of reference questions and questioning, Patrick Penland explained over 25 years ago, "Talk is the very basis of the interview, [and] the [library media specialist] should deliberately see to it that the patron does most of the talking and most of the deciding of what will be talked about. Genuine listening is hard work and requires that the [library media specialist] be alert to all the verbal and nonverbal cues that occur. Interviewing involves the hearing of the way things are being said, the tones used, the expressions and gestures employed" (424). Defining what is being asked and how to negotiate it is at the heart of the questioning process. Successful questioning requires active listening. This involves paying close attention to all that the student is saying. As a school library media specialist, you must become involved in the communications process; ascertain what the student wants to know.

Three basic purposes of reference interview questioning are:

■ To ascertain what information the student wants,

■ To clarify the question (what it really means), and

■ To discover the amount, level, and difficulty of the resources that will answer the question.

These purposes require the school library media specialist to carry on a conversation and to have time for such a dialogue. During the questioning procedure, it is important for the library media specialist to determine:

■ Why the question is being asked,

■ What the subject of the question is,

■ What the student already knows about the subject,

■ What information is required to answer the question: the amount and format,

■ What the barriers are to answering the question (time, available resources), and

■ What will be the most efficient and effective search strategy.

There are two major types of questions, open and closed. Open questions require the student to describe the need and its context. These questions frequently begin with *what, where,* and *how.* Open questions encourage further discussion. Closed questions, on the other hand, typically require the student to answer with "either-or." These questions usually involve a prior judgment by the library media specialist. Open and closed questions will often intermingle in the course of the reference interview.

Once the mode of questioning is established, the search for information proceeds. The school library media specialist should find out from the student not only the information he needs but also when he needs it and in what format. At that point, the reference interview departs from other types of library transactions. As a *school library media specialist*, it is your job to encourage the student's own research skills. Allow the *student* to conduct the search and locate the information to the best of his or her ability—and thus become information-literate. To paraphrase a portion of *Information Power's Information Literacy Standards for Student Learning*, the information-literate student should:

■ Access information efficiently and effectively,

■ Evaluate information critically and completely, and

■ Use information accurately and completely.

Successful interviewing techniques lead the student to appropriate and accurate resources and foster his or her information literacy skills for lifelong learning.

A successful reference interview, conducted using the most skilled questioning techniques, may not conclude with the full and precise answer to the student's question. However, if the student feels satisfied that she or he has been given adequate attention and has been directed to accurate resources, the interview was, indeed, a success.

Types of Reference Interviews

Not only does the school library media specialist need to ask appropriate questions, he or she must also make efficient use of time. This involves understanding the three most common types of reference interviews in the school library media center: ready-reference, research projects, and readers' advisory.

Ready-reference interviews include questions requiring short, factual answers, usually received from basic resources such as directories, encyclopedias, almanacs, dictionaries, and handbooks, both print and nonprint. The goal in ready-reference is to provide brief and accurate information—quickly.

Research project interviews lie at the other end of the spectrum. These questions involve in-depth coverage of a topic and often require the use of multiple sources of information. Research project questions may necessitate several interactions with the student over a period of time to reach the desired answers. The library media specialist's goal is to provide the student with the most adequate materials, then to explain and encourage information literacy skills.

Readers' advisory interviews are usually requests for "good" leisure reading. As a library media specialist, you must identify what the student considers "good" as well as select materials that conform to that definition. Of course, this is possible only with a current, comprehensive knowledge of the collection in your library media center, as well as a general knowledge of your school community. When conducting readers' advisory interviews, the library media specialist asks questions like:

■ "What do you enjoy reading?"

■ "What do you *not* like to read?"

■ "Do you enjoy reading long books or short stories?"

■ "Do you prefer reading a particular genre?"

■ "Do you have a favorite author?"

For younger students, showing them a variety of books and allowing them time to preview the materials works well. It is also best to offer several choices and, if possible, to provide a brief summary of the book or a "booktalk."

Sometimes described as a "different type" of reference interview is computer database searches. In this technological age, many, if not most, searches will require online information. Therefore, one of the school library media specialist's major goals is to locate the appropriate software and technologies and to help students learn proper searching procedures. Still another function in the reference interview process is to help students evaluate electronically retrieved information. (See Chapter 10 for a more complete discussion of technologies and reference services.)

Conclusion

The reference interview is an essential role of the school library media specialist. With the advent of new technologies in the school library media center have come a new pattern of service and a new approach to reference interviewing. However, the "basics" of reference services and questioning remain unchanged. The reference interview still involves human relations, communications, and interaction with the student. Good judgment and exceptional knowledge of resources remain imperative. The reference interview, in the past, present and future, connects knowledge with a student's information needs.

PART 4

Reference for the
New Millennium

Chapter **10**

Reference Skills in the Age of Technology

Introduction

The emergence of new, innovative technologies over the past few decades has altered virtually every aspect of school library media services. Reference skills, sources, and services are but one area that must be changed to meet the present-day needs of students in our global society. This chapter discusses technologies and how they affect various aspects of reference sources and services for school library media specialists.

The day of seeking answers has not ended. Only the process has changed. Accessing electronic information has two basic dimensions that distinguish it from print materials. The first is an almost unlimited storage capacity that continually expands. The second is the ability to extract from an enormous assemblage of data only what is needed. Mass storage and specific retrieval are both a blessing and a curse. The blessing is evident, but consider the curse. Masses of undifferentiated information are stored, which means that there may be thousands of citations for any given topic. The problem is finding the desired information from among the heaps of data. As school library media specialists, you now must become the "trained magicians" who are able to extract (or help the student extract) the specific information he or she needs. Today, students certainly have access to more information, but this does not necessarily mean that they have more knowledge. Is anyone the wiser because of the availability of limitless information?

Before computer technology advancements in the late 1960s, the method most school library media specialists used to find information was to consult a standard print reference work. Electronic resources (reference works in machine-readable form, computerized files of information) are searched in much the same way one would look for answers in print materials. The essential difference is that the technology offers numerous added avenues and methods of searching. Instead of depending on assigned subject headings, one may use a wide variety of approaches to gain the needed information. With the availability of electronic resources, the speed of searching has undoubtedly increased as well. Nonetheless, speedy *and* accurate searches are possible only if the library media specialist (and, hence, the student) knows how to use modern technologies.

An electronic work may be different in format from print sources, but it remains essentially the same in purpose and scope. New technologies serve the laudable purposes of making steps easier, considerably more efficient, and certainly more comprehensive. It is critically important for a library media specialist to know when to turn to print resources, when to use databases or the Internet, and when to avoid them all in favor of consulting an expert in the field. The goal is the same as it always has been: to locate correct information for students in the most efficient and effective manner possible.

Electronic Resources and Information Delivery Systems

There are numerous means of gathering reference information electronically. The following are examples. *Databases* are simply files of information; *electronic* databases are files that have been computerized. Literally thousands of electronic databases are available for school library media centers today in every imaginable subject. *Bibliographic databases* are machine-readable forms of indexes. The "base record" in this type of database is a citation to a book or article; most correspond to a print index. Bibliographic databases cover a wide range of subjects and prove extremely valuable in reference services. Still another type of database is the full-text database. The base record in this form is the entire article, paper, or other document. Numerous newspapers and journals are now full-text databases; many include more than one journal in a single file. With a full-text database, one has rapid access to complete records of information—an essential reference tool for library media specialists.

A *bibliographical network* (or *bibliographic utility*, as it is sometimes called) places a massive number of catalogs at the fingertips of school library media specialists. Moving away from a philosophy of ownership to one of accessibility, bibliographic networks are large databases of shared cataloging information created by the combined efforts of large libraries, such as the Library of Congress. These networks are information vendors who provide centralized databases for libraries to catalog, share, and retrieve bibliographic information according to national or international bibliographic standards. They have, at the heart of their databases, a set of bibliographic records in machine-readable form, called MARC (Machine-Readable Cataloging) records.

Bibliographic networks serve three basic functions:

■ To furnish complete information about a given library material,

■ To give the definitive spelling of an author's or publisher's name, and

■ To indicate where the materials are located.

Two major bibliographic utilities in the United States are OCLC and RLIN. OCLC, the Online Computer Library Center, has the greatest number of members, from all types and sizes of libraries, of any of the bibliographical networks. Growing daily, OCLC supports a database of over 40 million books, films, reports, and monographs derived from the Library of Congress, along with merged catalogs of the member libraries. OCLC is a nonprofit service and research organization whose networks link more than 30,000 libraries in 65 countries. OCLC services assist libraries in locating, acquiring, cataloging, and lending library materials.

RLIN, or Research Libraries Information Network, is the upscale bibliographic network. In addition to records of the Ivy League universities, it includes records from the major research centers.

The advantages of shared cataloging are evident. Each time any library creates and catalogs an acquisition, the results of that endeavor are shared with other libraries, virtually instantaneously. The speed of information increases once again.

Another electronic resource for reference services that is a direct outgrowth of bibliographic utility is the local or system catalog. This catalog goes by several names, including OPAC (Online Public Access Catalog) and LIS (Library Information System). These catalogs are "public" as opposed to system-restricted. The advantage of local or system catalogs is the use of search engines, which use a fast, effective, easily understood search language and are capable of handling numerous users simultaneously. The major advantages are ease of use and enhanced access to numerous reference materials.

Online databases contain information that is transferred to hard discs (or their technological equivalents) and then "read" by being mounted on a computer. The library media center accesses online databases over a communication network using a phone line, modem, computer, monitor, or printer. Online retrieval systems are the primary delivery system for most electronic resources. In online systems, a "local" computer is used to communicate with large vendor-operated "host" computers, which may contain hundreds or thousands of databases. The term "online" indicates that both the local and the host computer are in active communication at the time of the search. There are three major advantages to online retrieval:

■ The computer can store an unlimited amount of information;

■ It can search very rapidly; and

■ Materials can be added to the database at any time.

The "compact disc-read-only memory," or *CD-ROM*, has been an important and widely used format of reference information for a number of years. The electronic storage medium is an optical disc produced and read by laser technology. CD-ROMs are capable of containing over 250,000 pages of information and can be formatted to include illustrations, music, animation, films, and sound. Compact size, relatively low price, and ease of use make the majority of CD-ROMs ideal for student reference work.

The products developed for CD-ROMs are numerous and varied. To keep abreast of the magnitude and diversity of CD-ROMs, school library media specialists must carefully evaluate and select products using the specific criteria described more thoroughly in Chapter 2. Numerous review journals and online sources such as *Libraryvideo.com* (**www.libraryvideo.com**) currently have CD-ROMs as their primary focus. This source includes 12,000 educational videos and CD-ROMs accessible by subject. CD-ROMs provide library media centers with much of the power of multiple indexes, at a fraction of the time and cost. CD-ROMs typically are user friendly, easily understood and implemented by school library media specialists and students.

One of the more recent technology innovations is the "digital video disc" or *DVD*. DVDs allow video to be compressed and stored digitally on compact discs for computer access. These discs hold up to 20 times as much information as CD-ROMs. Digital videodiscs offer digital storage and playback of full motion video. DVDs are the same physical size as a CD-ROM, but can hold enough data for four full-length films. They offer high-quality soundtracks, many hours of high-fidelity music, or several gigabytes of computer data. DVDs do for video what CD-ROMs did for music. They are a new, important, and exciting addition to library media center reference sources and services.

The Internet

The Internet is the most important change in electronic information reference services since the development of electronic resources themselves. The greatest contribution of the Internet is not the technology, as impressive as it may be, but the sense of connection it makes possible between individuals and groups. The Internet is not really a source of information, but rather a means of communication—the "ultimate" communication network.

With regard to reference services for school library media centers, the Internet is all about providing information. As the Internet grows and develops as a forum for the exchange of information, library media specialists need to be actively involved in this "new world." As explained in *Information Power*, "Technology is a primary tool used by [school library media specialists] to forge communications between the program and the learning community. Technology...refers to the theory and practice of design, development, utilization, management, and evaluation of processes and resources for learning. Internet links expand national boundaries to allow connection to an ever-broadening circle to enhance students' and others' learning" (128, 130).

The Internet is so vast that knowing what is available is literally impossible; it is growing and developing in many directions simultaneously. The nonhierarchical nature of the Internet can be a challenge and an opportunity for library media specialists and students. The Internet links thousands of other communication and data networks with one another and with individual users. The lack of standardization of the Internet, however, requires school library media specialists to invest a great deal of time and energy in learning the variations of most importance to the library and student population. It is certain that terminology and resource formats will become more standardized in the years ahead.

However, with each new development and innovation in information technology, library media specialists face yet another challenge. Each new technology provides answers that previous technologies did not or could not provide. Each new technology also brings its own set of problems and dilemmas—all seeking solutions, although they may currently be hidden or obscure. How can school library media specialists invest time, energy, and money in a new technology to gain the advantages it offers without wasting some of those resources now and in the future? All one can feasibly do is gain experience, wisdom, and knowledge and try to envision the future. School library media specialists must gamble on the premise that the gains will outweigh the early fears and frustrations.

So where do you, as library media specialists, fit into this innovative process? You must help students use this resource, the Internet, effectively and efficiently.

You must educate information-literate students who can access, evaluate, and use electronic information for tomorrow's world. As time progresses, there will be more roles for school library media specialists, but it will take imagination, ingenuity, and much hard work. Success does not come easily.

As a school library media specialist, you can employ several methods to integrate the Internet into school library media reference services. One technique is to develop and maintain a library reference Web page. This Internet site should include an organized set of useful reference links. Three excellent Web sites of this nature include: *The Internet Public Library* (**www.ipl.org**); *The Virtual Reference Library at the Internet School Library Media Center* (**http://falcon.jmu.edu/~ramseyil/referenc.htm**); and *Dewey Browse* (**www.sau29.k12.nh.us/library/Dewey/dewey_browse_2.html**).

As a school library media specialist, you could provide training sessions regarding effective Web searching skills and strategies to students, teachers, and staff. You might even offer to answer reference questions via e-mail! Other possibilities—practical examples of Internet use in the area of reference services—will suggest themselves. You are limited only by your imagination and creativity.

School Library Media Reference Services: Looking Beyond

It is obvious to anyone walking into a school library media center that things have changed—most obviously, its physical appearance. Access, location, use, and evaluation of information have turned on its "electronic brain." As school library media specialists, we must embrace the changes, not resist them. We must move forward to make the school library media centers of tomorrow purposeful and exciting. We must make information-gathering effective and efficient—and enjoy it along the way! The rewards will be widespread. As the well-known simile goes, "Opportunities are like sunrises. If you miss them, they are gone." This is the case with technologies in the world of reference sources and services for school library media specialists.

Without a doubt, electronic and online reference resources will eventually replace the majority of print materials. Increased networking and cooperation between school library media centers and the community at large mean that distinctions between libraries and other sources of information will disappear. One misconception is that in the future there will be less dependence on the physical library media center. Why less? Information needs are growing and becoming more complex. The result is that there will be an *increased* need for "experts," school library media specialists with skills in searching, accessing, using, and evaluating information efficiently and effectively. In addition, students will, now more than ever before, need to be taught information literacy skills. Who better to teach them than the school library media specialist?

PART 5

Scenarios:

Situations for

School Library

Media Specialists

Introduction

It has been said that experience is the best teacher. With that in mind, the following three chapters are presented as the "next best thing," an aid in the form of *reference scenarios*.

Three primary reference functions of school library media specialists are:

■ Readers' information service

■ Evaluation and selection of reference materials

■ User instruction

Readers' Information Service involves extremely delicate forms of assistance. As a school library media specialist, you are walking a thin line between reference and readers' service, which is what you are doing when you answer such questions as:

■ What is a "good" book on AIDS?

■ What is the "best" novel to read?

■ Will you give me the funniest book you have in the library?

■ Will you find a book about sex education (for a friend)?

To complicate matters further, as a library media specialist you are also involved with the diverse and complicated issues of confidentiality and censorship.

Evaluation and Selection of Reference Materials is a highly individualized process. No two library media specialists will approach these in precisely the same manner. However, one universal, critical rule in evaluating and selecting resources for your library media center is knowledge of the needs (both known and anticipated) of your users. In addition, as a library media specialist, you must consider not only the user (student), but the community, administration, parents, teachers, and staff with whom you work. It is a complex—and extremely significant—job.

Unlike *user instruction* in public and academic libraries, *user instruction* for students is an essential, critical component of the school library media center. School library media specialists do not have the luxury of *not* providing comprehensive training in the basic sources and services of the library media center— the effective teaching of library skills. Indeed, it is time-consuming; however, without it, little time is available for other services.

In light of these three categories, the following chapters are intended to give the prospective (or even the experienced) school library media specialist insight into the numerous situations that may arise in a library media center. The scenarios are designed to provide a glimpse into the world of reference services. These chapters encompass both large and small library media centers in urban and rural settings. The situations include both practical and philosophical aspects of reference services for school library media specialists.

Chapter 11 covers issues specific to elementary school library media centers, whereas Chapter 12 speaks to the middle school library media center, and Chapter 13 presents scenarios one might encounter in the high school library media center. It is the author's hope that you will thoughtfully read, ponder, and discuss these scenarios with other prospective or experienced school library media specialists.

Following each situation is a list of questions to consider and reflect upon. As there is no one right solution for these problems, no answers are given. These scenarios are intended to foster discussions that will search the very heart of reference services for school library media specialists of the 21st century.

Special Notes for Instructors

The following scenarios are a means of eliciting discussion among prospective school library media specialists in the university or college classroom setting. The questions following each scenario are included merely to promote thoughtful conversation. As the instructor of the course, *your mission is to guide discussion*, as well as creative and critical thinking, based on your knowledge, experience, and insights. The questions are simply a *tool to encourage in-depth thought* about specific reference processes and services. These scenarios could also be used to guide student discussion in Web-enhanced or Web-based courses. In addition, technologies could be used; for instance, students could e-mail other classmates and experienced librarians about the situations prior to in-class discussions.

Adequate, relevant, and creative discussion will occur only with your expert guidance and direction.

Although some of the questions following each scenario can be answered with a simple "yes" or "no," you may elicit deeper conversations by asking questions such as:

- "Why or why not . . . ?"
- "What if . . . ?"
- "What might happen if . . . ?"
- "Are there alternatives; if so, what are they?"
- "Can you give another example?"
- "What ideas can you add to this?"
- "Why is this significant?"
- "Do you agree or disagree; why or why not?"
- "Will you elaborate further?"
- "What would *you* do in this situation? Why?"
- "What specific documents could be used to assist in this situation?"
- "Are there more ways than one to solve this problem? What are they?"
- "Have you observed this problem actually occurring? How was it handled?"
- "How might the answer alter due to differences in school setting, administration, or student population?"

Do not let the discussion be confined to questions and answers. A variety of helpful teaching strategies can be devised using scenarios or case histories. Examples of exercises for use in the classroom include

- Use role-playing.
- Think-pair-share: Give students time to think, discuss with a partner, and present their conclusion to the class.
- Ask a student to summarize another's point or response.
- Have students describe how they arrived at an answer.

- Play devil's advocate: Ask students to defend their reasoning against contrary points of view.
- Ask students to create their own questions or scenarios.
- Have students write their responses on paper, pass their unsigned papers to classmates to respond to each others' answers.

As instructor, you are the key to eliciting the desired discussions. The scenarios and questions simply *initiate* the process. You are limited only by your creativity and imagination.

Chapter *11*

Reference Scenarios for Elementary School Librarians

Scenario One: *How Much Is Enough?*

Providence Elementary school library media center has always worked with a meager budget. Miss Danielle Edge works diligently to help all students with their research projects, but the library rarely has enough materials to meet their reference needs. Danielle purchases the books carefully, always considering input from the teachers. In addition, she holds book fairs and has organized several other activities to supplement the reference collection and keep it as current as possible. But despite her hard work, the collection is not adequate to meet the requirements of all students.

Miss Edge recently received a request from a new teacher at Providence, Mrs. Jaffar, for materials concerning astronauts. Danielle accumulates individual biographies and prints out several encyclopedia and journal articles as well as information from the Internet. She collects approximately 30 reference materials and places them on reserve for Mrs. Jaffar.

Mrs. Jaffar is pleased with the results but explains to Miss Edge that there will be 115 students writing papers about individual astronauts. She would like for Danielle to keep them on reserve until all of the students have had the opportunity to write their papers. Miss Edge believes that this is unrealistic and unfair to the other students because these materials could be out of circulation for a long period of time.

Questions:

1. Is Miss Edge correct in believing this is an unrealistic and unfair request?
2. Is Mrs. Jaffar within her rights to make such a request?
3. Is there a way to handle this request without being unfair to other Providence Elementary students?
4. What are some other possible means of obtaining materials for Mrs. Jaffar?

5. What should Danielle say to Mrs. Jaffar?

6. Should she ask the administration for advice?

7. What do you think the real problem is in this scenario?

Scenario Two: *Picture Problems*

Having worked as a primary teacher for 15 years prior to becoming the library media specialist at Georgetown Elementary, Ms. Lucy Richardson has accumulated a wonderful collection of fiction and nonfiction materials for the kindergarten through third grades. Lucy is very fond of and familiar with primary resources. All the kindergarten through third grade teachers bring their classes to the media center frequently. Ms. Richardson holds wonderful story hours, gives exciting library instruction, and helps the primary students and teachers in every way possible.

Mr. Basma, a new fourth grade teacher at Georgetown, asks Lucy to prepare a collection of materials for his health classes dealing with the human body, growth, and nutrition. Ms. Richardson is not particularly interested in this assignment but manages to quickly put together a number of books and several copies of encyclopedia articles. She places the materials on a cart and sends them to Mr. Basma's classroom. He thanks her for the resources and proceeds with explaining his assignment to the students.

The next morning, two disconcerted mothers greet Mr. Basma. They place a book in front of him, open to a page with pictures of naked women and men, accompanied by an explicit diagram. Mr. Basma is surprised and embarrassed. He apologizes profusely to the mothers and storms into the library media center to see Ms. Richardson.

Questions:

1. Was this incident Lucy's fault?

2. Should she have screened the materials more closely?

3. Was it Mr. Basma's responsibility to preview the materials prior to giving them to the students?

4. Are pictures such as this inappropriate for an elementary school library media center?

5. If Ms. Richardson had been more interested in resources for the upper elementary students, would this incident have happened?

6. Should she have a written policy regarding a situation of this type?

7. What should Mr. Basma and Ms. Richardson say to the mothers?

8. What do you think the real problem is in this scenario?

Scenario Three: *Too Much Technology?*

Mr. Russ Miracle has worked on a technology grant for the St. Francis Elementary school library media center for two years. One month ago he received word that his dream had come true; he was given more than $5,000 for software for the library. Since that time, Mr. Miracle, having previously researched the software he would purchase should the grant be accepted, has scurried around purchasing numerous CD-ROMs. He bought CD-ROM encyclopedias as well as other CD-ROMs on subjects varying from animals to U.S. presidents. He now has 12 new, exciting CD-ROMs for the St. Francis media center.

Russ sends a memo to the teachers explaining his new purchases and inviting them to a demonstration after school on Monday afternoon. Many teachers attend, anxious to see the new materials. They are extremely excited and pleased with the purchases. Immediately, they begin bringing their classes to the library to use the new software.

Very quickly, Mr. Miracle, having only four computers capable of running the CD-ROMS, realizes there is a problem. All of the students want to use the "fun and exciting" technology; the computer area becomes chaotic. Russ is forced to limit the time and usage of the new software. The students and teachers are upset, stating that he should have thought of the problem before buying the CD-ROMs.

Questions:

1. Was Mr. Miracle wrong in applying for the grant to purchase CD-ROMs for the library media center?

2. What could he have done to avoid this problem (after purchasing the CD-ROMs)?

3. Should the teachers and students have been upset?

4. Should Mr. Miracle have asked for the teachers' help prior to buying the new technology?

5. Would it have been better for Russ to wait until he had enough computers before telling the teachers about the CD-ROMs?

6. What do you think the real problem is in this scenario?

Scenario Four: *Who Decides?*

Caroline Westjordan has been the library media specialist at Atherton Elementary for two years. Prior to her assignment there, Norman Woolridge had been the media specialist for three years. Caroline learned over the summer that Norman had died of cancer. He had served in the Gulf War and had received numerous military honors. The Woolridge family, upon his death, wished to establish a memorial to the soldiers in the Gulf War at the Atherton library media center. They donated $6,000 for a collection of materials about veterans of the Gulf War and a plaque honoring Norman Woolridge to be placed above the materials.

Mrs. Westjordan did not know Mr. Woolridge personally but was pleased that a donation was being given to Atherton Elementary. It was Caroline's responsibility to select the designated materials. The family would then review her choices prior to purchase.

Caroline felt that the materials should align with the curriculum at Atherton. She searched numerous journals and other selection sources, prepared a list of print and nonprint resources, and took the list to the Woolridge family for approval. To her dismay, the Woolridges explained that the materials were not acceptable. They felt that they were too "immature"; they wanted the collection to be a "scholarly" assortment of books dealing with the Gulf area, lists of veterans of war, and the like. Mrs. Westjordan was confused. She knew that the materials the Woolridge family wanted would be of no use to the students at Atherton Elementary.

Questions:

1. What should Caroline say to the Woolridge family?

2. Is it the right of the Woolridge family to approve the materials, regardless of their appropriateness?

3. Should there be a policy regarding donations and selection of materials at the Atherton library media center?

4. Should Mrs. Westjordan elicit the assistance of the administration?

5. Should Caroline refuse the materials, stating that they would not be appropriate for the library media center?

6. Should the selection have been discussed prior to the Woolridge family's approval?

7. What do you think the real problem is in this scenario?

Chapter **12**

Reference Scenarios for Middle School Librarians

Scenario One: *The Point of PowerPoint*

Hazelwood Middle School, a rural, middle-to-low-income school, until this year had the same library media specialist through all of its 30 years of existence. Joe Ball, the newly appointed library media specialist, just received his degree from a large university with a renowned library program. Joe has numerous innovative and progressive ideas for Hazelwood. He spent several weeks during the summer in the library media center preparing for the beginning of the school year.

While he was working in the library, a number of students stopped by the library media center to talk with and help him. One of his ideas for the beginning of school was to have students create a PowerPoint presentation as an orientation to the media center's reference sources and services. Joe believes that this will create student involvement and learning, as well as save him the time it would take to orient each class to reference materials and services.

Just after the beginning of school, Mr. Ball asked 20 students, all of whom he had met during the summer, to begin on the PowerPoint presentation. The students were excited to work with the technologies and eager to begin. Joe showed them how to create such a presentation and thoroughly explained the reference materials and related information. The students worked diligently for several weeks, creating an excellent presentation explaining reference sources and activities at Hazelwood library media center.

Mr. Ball then sent a memo to all of the teachers, asking them to bring their classes to the media center for an orientation about reference sources and services. The teachers were pleased that the students would learn about these materials. The following Monday, four teachers brought their classes to the library media center for the orientation.

At the end of the day, the four teachers, along with Hazelwood's principal, Mrs. Barker, came to see Mr. Ball. They expressed their displeasure with the

PowerPoint presentation, stating that he should have performed the orientation. In addition, they did not think creating the presentation was an appropriate or useful activity for the students. Mrs. Barker instructed Joe to complete the reference orientations himself. Joe felt that what he had done benefited the students and was completely appropriate for a middle school library media center.

Questions:

1. Is a PowerPoint presentation on reference sources and services appropriate or adequate for a middle school library media center?

2. Was it appropriate for Mr. Ball to use students to create such a presentation?

3. Did the students actually benefit from such an experience?

4. Should Mr. Ball introduce his innovative ideas more gradually?

5. Should Joe have told the teachers and principal about this presentation prior to showing it?

6. Should he have asked permission for the 20 students to create this presentation?

7. What should Mr. Ball say to the teachers? to Mrs. Barker?

8. Should he elicit the help of the students in explaining the benefits of creating such a presentation?

9. What do you think the real problem is in this scenario?

Scenario Two: *Reading Is Reading*

Tonja Hester, the school library media specialist at Doss Middle School, spends a great deal of time promoting the love of reading. Doss, situated in a rural, low-income area, has minimal funding for school library media materials. Many of the students who attend Doss are not reading at grade level; several have clearly defined reading difficulties. Over the previous four years, Tonja has supplemented the fiction collection by purchasing second-hand books, buying from publisher overstocks, and taking advantage of other bargains. She has also instituted various programs to encourage the students to read, with positive results. She has purchased many high-interest, low-ability books that are popular with the students and are much used. Because of Tonja, the Doss library media center is highly utilized by students who are eager and anxious to read.

Miss Hester stands firm in her belief that reading is the important issue; what is read is of less concern. Over the summer break, Tonja visited her parents in a nearby town, where she patronized numerous yard sales and flea markets, buying inexpensive reading matter (including comic books) she knew the students at Doss would enjoy in the fall.

Prior to the beginning of the school year, Tonja redecorated the leisure reading area, covering the walls with bright posters, placing comfortable chairs near the windows, and arranging the new acquisitions in clever displays. As Tonja expected, the students were pleased to have new reading materials. The comic books were a big hit; many students who rarely visited the media center enjoyed reading the comics in the new reading area.

Mrs. Fisher, a sixth grade language arts teacher, came storming into the library media center after school one Friday, waving several comic books in her hands. She claimed that she had found them in one of her student's folders, and that the student said he had gotten them from the media center. Mrs. Fisher was outraged to discover that comic books were in the library media center. She ripped the comics in half and stormed toward the principal's office. Miss Hester was too surprised and upset to utter a word.

Questions:

1. Was Miss Hester wrong to have comic books in the school library media center?
2. Is the *love of reading* more important than *what* is read?
3. Should Tonja have told the principal and teachers about her new purchases?
4. Should Doss have a written policy regarding the selection and purchase of library materials?
5. Were Mrs. Fisher's actions appropriate?
6. What should Miss Hester have said to Mrs. Fisher? To the principal?
7. Should she ask the students to help her "keep" her materials?
8. What is the real problem in this scenario?

Scenario Three: *Social Information Science*

Miss Mary Pat Simon has been the library media specialist at Fairdale Middle School for the past three years. She is a sensitive, energetic person and is well respected by the teachers and students. Fairdale is located in an urban, low-income area. Many of the students are from broken homes; drugs are prevalent in the school and community. Several students belong to gangs, and violence is an every-day occurrence.

Mary Pat recently read about a new concept in school media librarianship called Social Information (SI) Science. SI Science, she learned, is a strategy of dealing with students' problems through information and literature. By reading and learning, students can gain an understanding of their problems and be better able to cope with them.

Realizing many students at Fairdale Middle School have home, societal, and personal problems, Miss Simon decided to create a SI area with books, copies of relevant literature, and printouts from CD-ROMs and the Internet arranged by subject (divorce, drug and alcohol abuse, AIDS, gangs, violence, and similar problems).

As students visit the library media center, Mary Pat explains the new area; occasionally students share their problems with her. As the weeks pass, many students are locating and checking out materials about their problems. Mary Pat is thrilled; she believes that she has finally discovered a method of helping the students at Fairdale Middle School.

Questions:

1. Is it appropriate for a school library media specialist to assist students with personal problems?

2. What are potential difficulties that might arise out of this situation?

3. Should Miss Simon have discussed her new idea and SI area prior to implementing it?

4. Should *Social Information Science* be a part of school media librarianship?

5. Do you believe that students are really helped by reading about their problems?

6. Is Miss Simon within her legal rights to create a SI area? To discuss problems with students?

7. Is there any potential problem in this scenario? If so, what is it?

Scenario Four: *Evaluation of Electronic Information*

The Glovett Middle School, a wealthy independent school located in the Southeast, is blessed with all of the latest technologies. Ken Westley, library media specialist at Glovett for the past nine years, enjoys the large, modern, "hi-tech" media center in which he works. Students at Glovett utilize the library media center frequently with their classes as well as independently. They do much of their research on computers, in particular the Internet.

Over the years, Ken has become more and more concerned about the validity of materials obtained from the Internet. He decides to create criteria for evaluating the information. He develops an instrument titled *Evaluation of Electronic Information*, which consists of seven criteria to be used to determine if information obtained via the Internet is authentic: accuracy, authority, bias, content, permanence, presentation and organization, and timeliness. Ken distributes the Evaluation of Electronic Information to all teachers and staff with a note explaining what it is for and how it is to be used.

At the monthly faculty meeting following the distribution of Mr. Westley's evaluation criteria, many teachers explain that they appreciate his concern and hard work, but that the evaluation is much too difficult and time-consuming for their students to use. Ken explains that he will assist them and the students; that this is a critical issue that they, too, should be concerned about.

Questions:

1. Is Mr. Westley correct in stating that there is a need for specific criteria to evaluate electronic information?

2. Could he have approached this situation in a manner that would have "won the teachers over"?

3. Is it realistic to believe that middle school students would follow seven criteria before selecting "truthful" information from the Internet?

4. Is there an easier way in which they could determine accuracy of electronic information?

5. What should Mr. Westley have said to the teachers?

6. Should he ask the administration for their support?

7. What do you think the real problem is in this scenario?

Chapter **13**

Reference Scenarios for High School Librarians

Scenario One: *Is This a Language Problem?*

St. Christopher's High School is located in a low-to-middle-income, rural area just north of the Mexican border; most of the students at this school speak English as a second language. Constanza Vasquez, the school library media specialist at St. Christopher's for the past two years, is concerned that the majority of students are not using the library media center due to the language problem. She realizes the importance of the school library media center for these students; it could and should be a critical aid to their acquisition of English language skills.

Ms. Vasquez, being the resourceful person she is, recently discovered numerous free or inexpensive materials to help overcome this problem. Over the previous summer, she accumulated several Spanish-English dictionaries, some textbooks of varying levels, numerous high-interest, low-ability fiction books, and a number of instructional audiotapes. She even received two CD-ROMs containing basic English vocabulary and sentence structure.

At the beginning of the school year, Ms. Vasquez created an English Learning Resource Center (ELRC), where she displayed the books on a special shelf and placed a small table with comfortable chairs, several tape players with earphones, and two computers installed with the CD-ROMs in a cozy area at one side of the library media center. She even mounted bright, colorful posters in the ELRC area. She was quite proud of the results.

As students came into the media center at the beginning of the year, Constanza introduced them to the Resource Center and urged them to use it at their convenience. The students began visiting the ELRC before and after school; the numbers grew as the weeks passed. Many students appeared pleased with this new center, and Constanza felt it was working well, filling a void at the school.

One morning before the beginning of school, the principal, Mr. Noe, visited the library media center. He noticed a large group of students in this area, working at computers, listening to audiotapes, reading, and talking among themselves. Mr. Noe asked Ms. Vasquez what the students were doing. She proudly showed him the new English Learning Resource Center. To her surprise and dismay, Mr. Noe stated that this was not acceptable; that a "professional" should handle English language instruction. Mr. Noe told her either to distribute the materials among the four English teachers at St. Christopher's or catalog them and place them with the rest of the collection. Constanza stood saddened and confused.

Questions:

1. Should Ms. Vasquez have discussed her idea of the ELRC with Mr. Noe prior to assembling it?

2. Do you think Mr. Noe would have been in favor of this idea if Constanza had asked his permission before developing the center?

3. If Constanza must close the ELRC, should she distribute the materials to the English teachers or catalog them and place them with the rest of the collection?

4. What should Ms. Vasquez say to Mr. Noe?

5. Is there a way that Ms. Vasquez could keep the ELRC and please Mr. Noe as well?

6. Should she have discussed this issue with the teachers prior to beginning the ELRC?

7. Should she enlist the teachers' and students' assistance in keeping the center open?

8. Is her idea appropriate? Is it within her "rights" as a school library media specialist?

9. What do you think the real problem is in this scenario?

Scenario Two: *Does Technology Spell Success?*

Lafayette High School serves a suburban, upper-income area. The school library media center has all the latest technologies, of which the teachers and administration are very proud. The media center contains over 50 computers equipped with various CD-ROMs and the Internet. Many of the teachers send their classes to the media center to do research, most believing that their students merely need "access to the Internet" to locate information. The students enjoy "surfing the Net." Everyone seems pleased.

Mr. Hoad, the school library media specialist, is also proud of the modern, well-equipped library, but he is disturbed that students rarely use sources other than the Internet. He realizes that they can find much (and sometimes better) information in print resources and on CD-ROMs. He coaxes the students to look in other sources, but with little success. He eventually creates a "verbal library media center rule" that students are not to use the Internet before previewing other resources. He helps the students locate other research materials, but they are not interested. They disregard the rule, finding the Internet much more entertaining and exciting to use.

Finally, out of desperation, Mr. Hoad decides to take a more formal action. He sends a memo to the teachers, informing them that all students conducting research in the library media center must look at one other source (print, CD-ROM) before using the Internet.

The teachers and students are upset. They do not believe that it is Mr. Hoad's "right" to enforce such a rule. As a result, they boycott the media center. The principal, Ms. Sanders, is disturbed by this development and instructs Mr. Hoad to retract this rule with an apology and send another memo to the teachers stating that things will be as they were.

Questions:

1. Does Mr. Hoad have the right to enforce such a rule?
2. Did he handle this situation well? What could he have done instead?
3. Should the teachers and students have boycotted the library media center?
4. Could *they* have handled this situation better? How?
5. Did Mr. Sanders react appropriately?
6. Is there another, more effective manner in which Mr. Hoad could have enticed the students to use resources other than the Internet?
7. Is Mr. Hoad's rule an acceptable one for a school library media center?
8. Should Mr. Hoad have discussed the issue with Mr. Sanders or the teachers first?
9. What do you think the real problem is in this scenario?

Scenario Three: *Does Sex Belong in the School Library?*

Eva Price has been the library media specialist at Jefferson High School for the last 15 years. Jefferson High is a middle-to-high-income, suburban high school; she is blessed with much parent involvement and adequate funding and, after 15 years, has established a good rapport with many of the teachers in all curricular areas.

Mrs. Shaw, a biology teacher new to the school, recently assigned the students in her advanced biology class a research report dealing with any aspect of human reproduction. Although Ms. Price was aware of the assignment, Mrs. Shaw provided no detailed information.

Patrice, a senior and a frequent user of the library media center, asked Ms. Price to help her find information for her report. She wished to write about sexual activity of teenagers between the ages of 13 and 18. Mrs. Shaw gathered several books for Patrice and directed her to an appropriate CD-ROM as well as the Internet. Patrice began to work diligently; she remained in the media center until closing that day.

Several days later, Mrs. Shaw stormed into the library media center waving a sheet of paper. It was a printout she had found on Patrice's desk that contained information on sexual entertainment. Mrs. Shaw expressed her great displeasure and informed Eva that the administration would be alerted as to the "happenings" in the library media center. Taken by surprise, Ms. Price was at a loss for words.

Questions:

1. Was Ms. Price at fault for letting this information get into Patrice's hands?
2. What could she have done to avoid this situation?
3. Was Mrs. Shaw at fault in any way?
4. What documents could Ms. Price have provided to help her with this situation?
5. Is the school library media center responsible for all information retrieved?
6. Was Patrice at fault in any way?
7. Should Eva have remained with Patrice as she "surfed the Net" for information?
8. Was this topic of research appropriate for a high school biology class?
9. What should Ms. Price do first?
10. How could this situation have been avoided?

Scenario Four: *Talent Talks*

Kuldoon, a large high school, is situated in a small but progressive midwestern town. Kuldoon has been fortunate to have Mrs. Loretta Nash as their library media specialist for the previous 16 years. Energetic and creative, she has good rapport with teachers in all curriculum areas.

Two years ago, Loretta began a new program titled "Talent Talks." One week during the spring, she invites approximately 20 speakers to talk about their areas of expertise, ranging from architecture to horse racing. For that week, four to five speakers talk in the media center each day during a regularly scheduled class period. The speakers are experts in their field and, over the two years, have been extremely informational and entertaining.

Teachers at Kuldoon are invited to bring their classes to listen to the talks; individual students are given two "free passes," allowing them to hear speakers in whom they are particularly interested. Talent Talks has been a tremendous success; every speaker fills the media center to its 200-student capacity. The students appear to enjoy and learn from people talking about their careers and their lives. The free passes are much used.

This year, during the week of Talent Talks, the recently appointed principal, Mr. Lowe, has informed Mrs. Nash that he is concerned that students who attend the talks during their regularly scheduled class time "miss out" on academic lessons and that Talent Talks is detrimental to their formal education. He believes students are attending the talks to "get out of class." He tells Mrs. Nash to announce that this year will be the last year of Talent Talks. Loretta is upset. Mrs. Nash considers her program a success and does not wish to cancel it. She firmly believes Talent Talks has been and would continue to be beneficial to the students at Kuldoon High.

Questions:

1. Is "Talent Talks" a valid program for a school library media center?
2. Do students benefit from hearing outside speakers?
3. What should Loretta say to Mr. Lowe?

4. Should she end the free passes?

5. Is Mr. Lowe misinformed about this program?

6. Should Loretta elicit the students' help to maintain the program?

7. Should she ask the teachers to urge Mr. Lowe to let Talent Talks continue?

8. Does a program like this cause the library media specialist to neglect other media center duties?

9. How could Loretta have avoided this situation?

10. What do you think the real problem is in this scenario?

Appendix: Publisher Information

PUBLISHER	ADDRESS/PHONE/FAX	URL
ABC-CLIO	ABC-CLIO 130 Cremona Drive Santa Barbara, CA 93117 Phone: 1-805-968-1911 Toll Free: 1-800-368-6868 Fax: 1-800-685-9685	http://ABC-CLIO.com
Addison Wesley Longman	Addison Wesley Longman, Inc. One Jacob Way Reading, MA 01867-3999 Phone: 781.944.3700 Fax: 781.944.9338	http://www.awl.com/corp/
American Library Association	American Library Association 50 East Huron Street Chicago, IL 60611 Toll Free: 1-800-545-2433 Fax: 312.944.2641	http://www.ala.org/
American Psychological Association	American Psychological Association 750 First Street NE Washington, D.C. 20002-4242 Phone: 202.336.5500	http://www.apa.org/
Association of Educational Communications and Technology (AECT)	Association of Educational Communications and Technology 1800 N. Stonelake Dr., Suite 2 Bloomington, IN 47404 Phone: 812.335.7675 Fax: 812.335.7678	http://www.aect.org/
Belknap Press	Belknap Press/Harvard University Press Reference Library 79 Barden Treet Cambridge, MA 02138 Toll Free: 1-800-448-2242 Fax: 1-800-962-4983	http://www.hup.harvard.edu/
Britannica	Britannica 310 S. Michigan Ave. Chicago, IL 60604 Toll Free: 1-800-621-3900 Fax: 1-800-344-9624	http://www.eb.com
Brodart	Brodart 500 Arch Street Willamsburg, PA 17705 Intl. Phone: 570.326.2461 Fax: 1-800-999-6799	http://www.brodart.com

Cambridge University Press	Cambridge University Press Edinburgh Building Shaftesbury Road Cambridge CB2 2RU Phone: 44.0.1223.312393 Fax: 44.0.1223.315052	http://www.cup.cam.ac.uk/
Cassell Academic	Cassell Academic Wellington House 125 Strand, London WC2R 0BB Phone: 0171.420.5555 Fax: 0141.240.8531	http://www.cassell.co.uk/
Charles Scribner's Sons	Charles Scribner's Sons University of South Carolina Press 718 Devine St. Columbia, SC 29208 Toll Free: 1-800-768-2500 Fax: 1-800-868-0740	http://www.sc.edu/uscpress/
Checkmark Books	Checkmark Books Facts on File, Inc. 11 Penn Plaza, 15th Floor New York, NY 10001 Toll Free: 1-800-322-8755 Fax: 1-800-678-3633	http://www.checkmark.net/
College Board	The College Board 45 Columbus Avenue New York, NY 10023-6992 Phone: 212.713.8000	http://www.collegeboard.org/
Collier	Collier 919 Third Ave., 14th Floor New York, NY 10022 Phone: 212.508.6000 Fax: 212.508.6160	http://Collier.com
Columbia University Press	Columbia University Press 562 West 113th Street New York, NY 19925 Toll Free: 1-800-944-8648 Fax: 1-800-944-1844	http://www.cc.columbia.edu/cu/cup/
Compton's	Compton's Phone: 617.494.1200 Fax: 617.494.1219	http://www.comptons.com/
Dorling Kindersley	Dorling Kindersley 3 Chandos Place London WC2N 4HS United Kingdom Phone: 44.0.20.7753.7335 Fax: 44.0.20.7969.8027	http://www.dk.com/

EBSCO	EBSCO Division Headquarters Birmingham, AL Phone: 205.991.6600 Fax: 205.995.1518	http://EBSCO.com/home/
Facts on File	Facts on File 11 Penn Plaza, 15th Floor New York, NY 10001-2006 Toll Free: 1-800-322-8755 Fax: 1-800-678-3633	http://www.factsonfile.com/
Gale Group	The Gale Group 27500 Drake Road Farmington Hills, MI 48331 Toll Free: 1-800-877-GALE Fax: 1-800-414-5043	http://www.gale.com/
Government Printing Office	Government Printing Office P.O. Box 371954 Pittsburgh, PA 15250-7954 Phone: 202.783.3238 Fax: 202.512.2250	http://www.gpo.gov/
Grolier's, Inc.	Grolier's, Inc. 2925 Chemin Cote-de-Liesse Saint-Laurent, Quebec H4N 2X1 Toll Free: 1-800-353-3140	http://www.grolier.com/
H.W. Wilson	H. W. Wilson 950 University Avenue Bronx, NY 10452 Toll Free: 1-800-367-6770 Fax: 1-800-590-1617	http://www.hwwilson.com/
Hammond, Inc.	Hammond Corporation 95 Progress Street Union, NJ 07083 Toll Free: 1-800-526-4953	http://www.hammondmap.com/
HarperCollins	HarperCollins Publishers 1350 Avenue of the Americas New York, NY 10019-4703 Toll Free: 1-800-822-4090	http://www.harpercollins.com/
Hartley Courseware	Hartley Courseware 3451 Dunckel Road, Suite 200 Lansing, MI 48911 Phone: 517.394.8500 Toll Free: 1-800-247-1380 Fax: 517.394.9899	http://www.nol.net/~athel/org/ har.html
Harvard University Press	Harvard University Press 79 Garden Street Cambridge MA 02138 Toll Free: 1-800-448-2242 Fax: 1-800-962-4983	http://www.hup.harvard.edu/

The Horn Book	The Horn Book, Inc. 56 Roland Street, Suite 200 Boston, MA 02129 Toll Free: 1-800-325-1170 Fax: 617.628.0882	http://www.hbook.com/
Houghton Mifflin	Houghton Mifflin Riverside Publishing 425 Spring Lake Drive Itasca, IL 60143-2079 Toll Free: 1-800-323-9540	http://www.hmco.com/
IDG Books Worldwide	IDG Books Worldwide, Inc. 919 E. Hillsdale Blvd., Suite 400 Foster City, CA 94404-2112 Toll Free: 1-800-762-2974	http://www.idgbooks.com/
Intermedia	Intermedia Information Services, Inc. 13103 Anvil Place Suite 204 Herndon, VA 20171 Phone: 703.478.2277 Fax: 703.478.6656	http://www.i-media.com/
Libraries Unlimited, Inc.	Libraries Unlimited, Inc. P.O. Box 6633 Englewood, CO 80155-6633 Toll Free: 1-800-237-6124 Fax: 303.220.8843	http://www.lu.com/
Linworth Publishing, Inc.	Linworth Publishing, Inc. 480 E. Wilson Bridge Rd, Suite L Worthington, OH 43085 Phone: 614.436.7107 Fax: 614.436.9490	http://www.linworth.com
Little, Brown, and Company	Little, Brown and Company 3 Center Plaza Boston, MA 02108-2084 Phone: 617.263.2810 Fax: 617.263.2863	http://www.twbookmark.com/
Merriam Webster	Merriam Webster, Inc. 47 Federal Street P.O. Box 281 Springfield, MA 01102 Phone: 413.734.3134 Fax: 413.731.5979	http://www.m-w.com/
Microsoft Corporation	Microsoft Corporation 5335 Wisconsin Ave. NW Suite 600 Washington, DC 20015 Phone: 202.895.2000 Fax: 202.364.8853	http://www.microsoftcorporation.com

Modern Language Association of America	Modern Language Assoc. of America 10 Astor Place New York, NY 10003 Phone: 212.475.9500	http://www.mla.org
Monarch Press	Monarch Press P.O. Box 366 Grass Lane, MI 49240 Phone: 888.283.6767 Fax: 888.517.7377	http://www.monarchpress.com/
National Geographic Society	National Geographic Society P.O. Box 11303 Des Moines, IA 50340 Toll Free: 1-800-437-5521 Fax: 1-515-362-3345	http://www.nationalgeographic.com
NewsBank	NewsBank 397 Main Street P.O. Box 1130 Chester, VT 05143 Toll Free: 1-800-243-7694	http://NewsBank.com/
Omnigraphics	Omnigraphics, Inc. 615 Griswold Detroit, MI 48226 Toll Free: 1-800-234-1340 Fax: 1-800-875-1340	http://www.omnigraphics.com/
Oryx Press	Oryx Press P.O. Box 33889 Phoenix, AZ 85067-3887 Toll Free: 1-800-279-6799	http://www.oryxpress.com/
Oxford University Press	Oxford University Press 2001 Evans Road Cary, NC 27513 Phone: 919.677.0977	http://www.oup-usa.org/
Prentice-Hall	Prentice-Hall One Lake Street Upper Saddle River, NJ 07458 Phone: 201.236.7156 Toll Free: 1-800-382-3419	http://www.prenhall.com/
Princeton University Press	Princeton University Press 41 William Street Princeton, NJ 08540-5237 Phone: 609.258.4900 Fax: 609.258.6305	http://www.pup.princeton.edu/
ProQuest	Bell & Howell Information and Learning 300 North Zeeb Road P.O. Box 1346 Ann Arbor, MI 48106-1346 Toll Free: 1-800-521-0600 Phone: 734.761.4700	http://www.ProQuest.com/

R. R. Bowker Co.	R. R. Bowker Co. 121 Chanlon Road New Providence, NJ 07974 Phone: 888.269.5372	http://www.bowker.com/
Rand McNally	Rand McNally 8255 N. Central Park Ave. Skokie, IL 60076 Toll Free: 1-800-275-7263	http://www.randmcnally.com/
Random House	Random House, Inc. 1540 Broadway New York, NY 10036 Phone: 212.782.9000 Fax: 212.302.7985 Toll Free: 1-800-726-0600	http://www.randomhouse.com/
Reed Reference Publishing	Reed Reference Publishing 121 Chanlon Rd. New Providence, NJ 07974 Toll Free: 1-800-521-8110	http://www.reedref.com/
St. James Press	Routledge/St. James Press 7625 Empire Drive Florence, KY 41042 Toll Free: 1-800-634-7064 Fax: 1-800-248-4724	http://www.routledge.com/ stjames/
St. Martins Press	St. Martins Press Oxford Road Manchester UK M13 9NR Phone: 44.0.161.273.5539 Fax: 44.0.161.274.3346	http://www.stmartins.com/
Salem Press	Salem Press Two University Plaza, Suite 121 Hackensack, NJ 07601 Toll Free: 1-800-221-1592 Fax: 201.968.1411	http://www.salempress.com/
Scarecrow Press	Scarecrow Press RLPG 67 Mowat Avenue, Suite 241 Toronto, ON Canada Phone: 416.534.1660 Fax: 416.534.3669	http://www.scarecrowpress.com/
Simon & Schuster	Simon & Schuster 1230 Avenue of the Americas New York, NY 10020 Toll Free: 1-800-331-6531	http://www.simonandschuster. com/
Times Books	Random House, Inc. 1540 Broadway New York, NY 10036 Phone: 212.782.9000 Fax: 212.302.7985 Toll Free: 1-800-726-0600	http://www.randomhouse.com/

University Microfilm International (UMI)	University Microfilm Intenational Bell & Howell 300 North Zeeb Road P.O. Box 1346 Ann Arbor, MI 48106-1346 Toll Free: 1-800-521-0600	http://www.umi.com/
William Morrow	William Morrow, an imprint of HarperCollins Publishers Marketing Dept. 1350 Avenue of the Americas New York, NY 10019 Phone: 212.473.1452	http://www.williammorrow.com/
World Book	World Book, Incorporated 233 N. Michigan Ave. Suite 2000 Chicago, IL 60601 Phone: 312.729.5800 Toll Free: 1-800-WORLDBK Fax: 312.729.5600	http://www.worldbook.com/
World Resources Institute	World Resources Institute 10 G Street, NE Suite 800 Washington, DC 20002 Phone: 202.729.7600 Fax: 202.729.7610	http://www.wri.org/

References

AASL and AECT. *Information Power: Building Partnerships for Learning.*
Chicago: American Library Association, 1988.

Eisenberg, Michael. "Big6 TIPS: Teaching Information Problem Solving:
Information Seeking Strategies." *Emergency Librarian.* 25 (1997): 22.

Katz, William. *Introduction to Reference Work: Information Sources.* 7th ed.
New York: McGraw-Hill, 1997.

Kuhlthau, Carol. "Inside the Search Process: Information Seeking from the User's
Perspectives." *Journal of the American Society for Information Science.*
42 (1991): 361-371.

Kuhlthau, Carol. "Learning in Digital Libraries: An Information Search Approach."
Library Trends. 45 (1997): 708-725.

Penland, Patrick. *Interviewing for Counselor and Reference Librarians.*
Pittsburgh, PA: University of Pittsburgh, 1970.

Pitts, Judy. "Six Research Lessons from the Other Side." *The Book Report.* 11
(1993): 22-24.

Strayer, Joseph, ed. *The ALA Glossary of Library and Information Science.*
Chicago: American Library Association, 1983.

Stripling, B. K., & Pitts, J. *Brainstorms and Blueprints: Teaching Library Research
as a Thinking Process.* Englewood, CO: Libraries Unlimited, 1988.

Whittaker, Kenneth. "Towards a Theory for Reference and Information Services."
Journal of Librarianship. 9 (1977): 49-63.

Woolls, Blanche. *The School Library Media Manager.* 2nd ed. Englewood, CO:
Libraries Unlimited, 1999.

Glossary

The following are simple definitions. They are not meant to replace more thorough definitions that can be located in various other reference sources.

Abridged (dictionary): A dictionary that is selectively compiled; typically based on a larger dictionary (between 130,000 and 265,000 words).

Abstract: An extension of an index that presents a brief, objective summary of the content and serves as an aid in assessing the contents of a document.

Almanac: A resource that provides useful data and statistics related to countries, personalities, events, and subjects.

Authority: The education and experience of the authors, editors, and contributors of a resource, as well as the reputation of the publisher or sponsoring agency.

Bibliographic Control: This term refers to two kinds of access to information: 1) bibliographic (Does the work exist?), and 2) physical (Where can the work be found?).

Bibliographic Database: Machine-readable forms of indexes.

Bibliographic Instruction: Any activity designed to teach students how to locate and use information.

Bibliographic Network: Information vendors who provide a centralized database for libraries to catalog, share, and retrieve bibliographic records according to national and international bibliographic standards.

Bibliographic Utilities: (*See* Bibliographic Network)

Bibliography: A list of materials or resources.

Big6 Information Problem-Solving Model: Developed by Michael Eisenberg and Robert Berkowitz, this is an information problem-solving model using six basic steps.

Biographical Source: A resource that provides information about people—from facts to pictures of their everyday lives.

CD-ROM: (Compact disc-read-only memory) An optical disc that is an electronic storage medium produced and read by means of laser technology. It is capable of containing over 250,000 pages of information.

Database: Files of information.

Dictionary: A resource containing words usually arranged along with information about their forms, pronunciations, functions, etymologies, meanings, and syntactical and idiomatic uses. A resource that alphabetically lists terms or names important to a particular subject or activity, along with discussion of their meaning and application.

Directory: A list of people or organizations listed in a systematic way; an alphabetical or classified list containing names and addresses.

DVD: (Digital video disc) Videos that are compressed and stored digitally on compact discs for computer access. DVDs are capable of holding up to 20 times as much information as CD-ROMs.

Electronic Database: Files of information that have been computerized.

Electronic Resources: Reference works in machine-readable forms; computerized files of information.

Encyclopedia: A work that contains information on all branches of knowledge or comprehensively treats a particular aspect of knowledge.

Gazetteers: Geographic dictionaries that provide information regarding geographic place-names.

Geographical Source: A resource used fundamentally to answer location questions, such as maps, atlases and gazetteers.

Handbook: (Also called manual) A resource that serves as a guide to a particular subject.

Index: An analysis of a document, typically by subject.

Information Literacy: The ability to access, comprehend, use, and evaluate information.

Library Catalog: A catalog that lists works located in a given library or libraries.

National Bibliography: A bibliography that lists materials published in a particular country and is often the product of the government.

National Union Catalog (NUC): The United States National Bibliography, which lists all works cataloged by the Library of Congress and other members of the system.

OCLC: (Online computer Library Center) A bibliographic network. OCLC has the greatest number of members and links to over 30,000 libraries in 65 countries.

OPAC: (Online Public Access Catalog) A public catalog (as opposed to system-restricted) that uses search engines.

Ready-Reference Questions: Questions that usually require only a single, typically uncomplicated, straightforward answer.

Reference Interview: A conversation between the librarian and the student for the purpose of clarifying and meeting the student's needs.

Reference Source: A material designed to be consulted for definite items of information rather than to be examined consecutively.

RLIN: (Research Libraries Information Network) A bibliographic network that includes records of the "Ivy League" universities and major research centers.

Scope: The purpose of the source and its intended audience—what is covered and in what detail.

Selection Policy: A policy that (ideally) explains the process followed and the priorities established before any resource is purchased and put into the school library media center collection.

Selection Tools: Resources (journals, books, electronic sources) that assist in the proper and efficient selection of materials for the school library media center.

Subject Bibliography: A bibliography that lists materials that relate to a specific topic.

Thesaurus: A specialized dictionary that deals solely with word synonyms and antonyms.

Trade Bibliography: A commercial publication that includes the necessary information to select and purchase recently published materials.

Unabridged (dictionary): A dictionary that attempts to include all of the words in the language at the time the dictionary is assembled (over 265,000 words).

Union Catalog: A catalog that identifies the materials held in more than one library.

Universal Bibliography: Everything published from the beginning through the present. (Time, territory, subject, language, or form does not limit it.)

Weeding: Selectively deleting irrelevant, out-of-date, unused, and poor-quality materials from the library media center collection.

Yearbook: A resource that presents facts and statistics for a single year.

Index